Jane Austen:

The Missing Pieces

Harvey T. Dearden

First published in paperback in Great Britain in 2020.

ISBN-13: 9798697782644

For Ottilie Elin

('Otts')

"May I ask to what these questions tend?'

"Merely to the illustration of your character,"
said she, endeavouring to shake off her gravity.
"I am trying to make it out."

"And what is your success?"

She shook her head. "I do not get on at all. I
hear such different accounts of you as puzzle
me exceedingly."

Pride and Prejudice, ch.18

CONTENTS

AUTHOR'S NOTE viii

TIMELINE ix

INTRODUCTION 1

1. WHAT WAS JANE LIKE? 3

2. JANE'S MAGIC 10

3. JANE'S MANNERS 18

4. INTERLUDE - JANE'S LIES 22

5. THE STING IN THE ENTAIL 25

6. THE TROUBLE WITH TOM 29

7. JANE'S LOVE LIFE 35

8. JANE'S PROPOSAL 39

9. JANE'S MARRIAGE 47

10. JANE'S DARK SIDE 54

11. CASSANDRA'S FIRE 60

12. CASSANDRA'S SELECTION 65

13. JANE'S DOOR 71

14. JANE'S VOICE 74

15. JANE'S CHAMBER POT 82

16. TWO LETTERS 87

17. JANE'S LABORATORY 90

18. JANE'S ORPHANS 94

19. JANE'S FACE 99

20. JANE'S GOD 107

21. JANE'S MANUSCRIPTS..112

22. INTERLUDE - JANE'S DEFINITIONS.................................118

23. JANE'S DEATH..121

24. JANE'S GRAVE..126

EPILOGUE – JANE *PERDONO*...137

APPENDIX 1: CHARLOTTE'S LETTERS 141

APPENDIX 2: JANE AUSTEN; ENGINEER?............. 144

INDEX...154

BIBLIOGRAPHY 151

ACKNOWLEDGEMENTS...157

ABOUT THE AUTHOR 158

AUTHOR'S NOTE

Jane Austen's novels are referred to by chapter numbers as they appear in any continuously numbered modern edition; thus *Emma*, ch. 45, not vol. 3, ch. 3.

I abbreviate the longer titled novels:

P&P – *Pride and Prejudice*

S&S – *Sense and Sensibility*

MP - *Mansfield Park*

NA - *Northanger Abbey*

All quotations from, and references to, Jane Austen's letters are taken from *Jane Austen's Letters*, ed. Deirdre Le Faye, 4th edition, OUP, Oxford, 2014; letters are identified throughout by letter number as assigned by Le Faye and by date.

References, which are given at the end of each chapter, are identified by a numeral in square brackets e.g., [1]. Footnotes by an alphabetic character in superscript e.g.[a]

TIMELINE

YEAR	PLACE	AGE	Lady Susan	E&M/S&S	F/P&P	Susan/NA	The Watsons	MP	Emma	Persuasion	Sanditon	# Letters	Events
1793	Steventon	17	S									-	
1794		18										-	
1795		19		S								-	
1796		20			S							7	Tom Lefroy flirtation
1797		21			R							-	Tom Fowle dies. Henry marries Eliza.
1798		22				S						9	
1799		23				F						6	
1800		24										6	
1801	↓	25										10	
1802	Bath	26										-	Bigg-Wither proposal
1803		27										-	
1804		28					S					1	Mrs Lefroy dies
1805		29	F				A					8	Father dies. Trafalgar.
1806	↓	30										1	
1807	S'pton	31										3	
1808		32										12	Mrs E. Austen (Knight) dies
1809	↓	33		F								8	'MAD' letter
1810		34										-	
1811	Chawton	35		P				S				6	Regency begins
1812		36			F							2	
1813		37			P			F				19	Eliza de Feuillide dies
1814		38						P	S-F			20	Mrs Charles Austen dies
1815		39							P	S		23	Waterloo
1816		40								F		14	Henry bankrupt
1817		41				P				P	S-A	14	Jane dies

S	Started	R	Rejected by publisher
F	Finished	P	Published
A	Abandoned		Copyright with Crosby
	Dormant/In-progress	↓	Moved

INTRODUCTION

I must declare from the outset that I am no scholar of literature (of engineering perhaps, but that is literally another book), and I do not attempt an exposition of the established history of Jane, which has been comprehensively covered by others. Similarly, you will find little by way of literary criticism. What you will find are a series of speculations on points where we do not have definitive answers. The starting point for these essays has been things we do *not* know about Jane: all the missing information; all the gaps in the record. For a gap may still tell us something. By exploring its outlines, we may come to an understanding of what may once have filled it. We may examine the surrounding patterns and attempt interpolation. (As we do with a jigsaw puzzle.)

I acknowledge that because this book largely inhabits the realm of speculation, I am spared the constraints of rigour imposed on the professional historian. I can imagine this might be galling to those so constrained. I sympathise, but it could be no other way if this book were to be. You might as well complain about the rain being wet…

It is often said that 'absence of evidence is not evidence of absence', but that is not necessarily true, for it might well substantiate the possibility. Medical students are taught, 'If you hear hoof beats, think horses, not zebras.' Instead, I look for likely explanations; I proceed primarily by logical *induction* rather than *deduction*.

I am emboldened in this enterprise by another truth that Jane would likely have endorsed (although this one is expressed without irony):

> 'It is universally acknowledged that there is a great uniformity among the actions of men, in all nations and ages, and that human nature remains still the same, in its principles and operations. The same motives always produce the same actions. The same events follow from the same causes. Ambition, avarice, self-love, vanity, friendship, generosity, public spirit; these passions, mixed in various degrees, and distributed through society, have been, from the beginning of the world, and still are, the source of all the actions and enterprises, which have ever been observed among mankind.'

> (David Hume, *An Enquiry Concerning Human Understanding*, 1748)

I do not insist (in the manner of Lady Russell) you should be persuaded, but I hope you will (in the manner of Mr. Darcy) be intrigued.

Harvey T. Dearden CEng

North Wales

WHAT WAS JANE LIKE?

We all have an idea, whether articulated or not. The point has been made before (most recently by Lucy Worsley in her book *Jane Austen at Home*) that in searching for Jane we each identify a personal interpretation rather than a definitively objective account. [1]

Would we have liked her in person? Would she have been a friend? We might be confident we would have been (are?[a]) a friend to her, but would she have been a friend to us?

There are some things that we can all immediately agree upon: intelligent, witty, perceptive, and possessing both sense and sensibility. Beyond that?

The epitaph engraved in Winchester Cathedral cites the 'benevolence of her heart' and her 'sweetness of temper'. I wonder?

---

[a] In evangelising on her behalf, on singing her praises to anyone that will stand still long enough, I feel we can claim to be her friend, although the worry is, that without a proper introduction, and a degree of intimacy beyond acquaintanceship, she would likely consider that an unpardonable liberty!

I am left with the impression that she would not suffer fools gladly. I can imagine a degree of forbearance in matters beyond any reasonable expectation of control, but she would likely have found importunate demands on her attention provoking; that is a cross the intelligent must bear when assailed by clamorous idiots, the question is rather how she would have reacted?

Her surviving correspondence reveals a sharp tongue, but this is sharpness as in cutting and incisive, rather than cruel and unfair. Her sharpness was a matter of private correspondence between herself and Cassandra; it was not wielded as a weapon outside of that world.

I can imagine a playful response when she was in the mood, amusing herself with wordplay; replies with layered meanings that would mostly fly above the heads of her interlocutors. I can imagine them accepting a reply at face value and then, as they turn away, realising that there may be more to the answer than first perceived. Jane then all innocence with the dullards with no real comprehension, and with a twinkle in her eye for those with a dawning realisation of being played with. And with an absolute joy if she found someone that could 'return her serve'! (How she would have loved a cryptic crossword! I could weep that she was so denied!)

It is clear she enjoyed the ridiculous and this would likely have given her some armour against the nonsense in the world. What cannot be cured must be endured. Or better still, laughed at. She would have been good humoured, in the sense that she was more ready to smile than frown. I have no sense of a fractious ill-tempered woman, continually displeased with the world and the people around her; it is inconceivable that such an afflicted creature could produce the delights that Jane did.

For the most part she must have been conscious of outclassing almost all those around her, with the 'extraordinary endowments of her mind'. [2] I see her finding her equals in her imagination. In looking for examples, most immediately, of course, we seize on the spirited Elizabeth Bennet, who redeems Darcy from a likely spiral of depression and increasingly remote isolation; Darcy himself, who spars with Elizabeth (Jane), and is both intrigued and intriguing; handsome, clever, rich Emma, for whom Jane explicitly declares her liking,[b] who is herself redeemed by realisation of her love for Mr Knightley; and in turn, Mr Knightley himself who mentors Emma and provides a model of unaffected propriety.

Jane was 'bookish' certainly, but not through any wish to avoid interaction with the world (I do not perceive an introvert) but rather because only in that realm could she really unfurl her wings. A healthy balance of extroversion and introversion, with behaviour tailored appropriately to the circumstances. Self-possessed, reflective, and comfortable with her own company; so very necessary for her to achieve what she did.

Discerning, certainly. For me, perhaps Jane's most defining aspect. The ability to make nice (meaning 'fine'; the proper meaning of the word) distinctions from 'the most thorough

---

[b] 'I am going to take a heroine whom no one but myself will much like.' (*A Memoir of Jane Austen* – J.E. Austen-Leigh)

knowledge of human nature'. [3] I do *not* accuse Jane of being 'nice' in terms of being pleasing. That, for me, carries an imputation of insipidness that I do not see as fitting Jane.

I see a woman that has a strong suspicion, based on that same 'thorough knowledge of human nature' that the men are talking balderdash, but being herself unsure of her footing, preferring to hold her tongue.

Her declarations concerning others' looks suggests she was neither vain nor despairing of her own.

At age 36, in a letter to Cassandra she reports herself as '...very well satisfied with his notice of me. '"A pleasing looking young woman"; - that must do; - one cannot pretend to anything better now – thankful to have it continued a few years longer!' [4]

She was scared of thunderstorms:

> 'We sat upstairs - & had Thunder & Lightening as usual. I never knew such a Spring for Thunder storms as it has been! – Thank God! – we have had no bad ones here. – I thought myself in luck to have my uncomfortable feelings shared by the Mistress of the House, as that procured Blinds & Candles.' [5]

She was right-handed (just in case you were wondering). At the end of a long letter she signs off with: 'Distribute the affec^te Love of a Heart not so tired as the right hand belonging to it. -' [6]

Loyal? Unfailingly.

Prim? No, no, no! See Chapter 153 'Jane's Chamber Pot'.

Proper? Well, yes, but not as typically associated with primness, which implies an unbending, unthinking insistence on etiquette and observance of social niceties. I imagine Jane as having the intelligence to adapt to circumstances and being able to 'bend the rules' to good effect whilst remaining true to the underlying principle of showing consideration for others. Adopting the 'right conduct' expounded in her books.

Jane as the boss? Struggling with the need to work with mediocrities. A 'completer-finisher' that finds it difficult to accept that good enough will do. Her sharp wits finding much to be sharp about and her female subordinates correspondingly resentful. Her male subordinates admonishing themselves at being found wanting and exerting themselves to greater efforts to secure a beneficent smile. Not the captain of a happy ship.

Jane as screenwriter? Capable certainly, but I wonder whether she would have been able to tolerate directorial deviations from her original intent?

Jane as author? What would she have written in our age? What style would she have adopted? I imagine she would have thoroughly enjoyed P. G. Wodehouse.

Rich Jane? Unlike the many whose dream lottery win yields cars, yachts, cruises, spending, bigger houses, Jane would likely dream simply of the personal time and space that a win would buy her.

Jane as Agony Aunt? Again, certainly capable; witness her correspondence with her niece Fanny. But unable to tolerate the clamorous idiots.

So, in summary, no saint ('Pictures of Perfection, as you know, make me sick and wicked' [7]), but certainly no sinner. Funny and, at times irreverent. A firm and faithful friend. Both blessed and cursed with incisive intelligence. The blessing is self-evident. The curse? The Cassandra-like[c] (!) ability to foresee how things could/should be, but with few ready to believe her, and the resentment of those less able (particularly women) who would be intimidated by that intelligence. Claire Harman gives this delicious 1815 report from Miss Mary Russell Mitford:

> 'A friend of mine, who visits her now, says that she has stiffened into the most perpendicular, precise, taciturn piece of "single blessedness" that ever existed, and that, till *Pride and Prejudice* showed what a precious gem was hidden in that unbending case, she was no more regarded in society than a poker or firescreen, or any other thin upright piece of wood or iron that fills its corner in peace and quietness. The case is very different now; she is still a poker – but a poker of whom everyone is afraid. It must be confessed that this silent observation from such an observer is rather formidable. Most writers are good-humoured chatterers – neither very wise nor very witty: - but nine times out of ten (at least in the

---

[c] Cassandra being the Greek priestess cursed to give true prophecies but never be believed.

very few that I have known) unaffected and pleasant, and quite removing by their conservation any awe that may have been excited by their works. But a wit, a delineator of character, who does not talk is terrific indeed!' [8]

It is impossible to know which of the first part of these words are due to Mary and which to her friend – they do show an independent intelligence, but is it misapplied? The intimidated might very well perceive 'stiffness' where others would see 'principled'.

REFERENCES

1. L. Worsley, *Jane Austen at Home*, Hodder & Stoughton, London, 2017, p. 4.
2. From the epitaph on her grave.
3. *NA*, ch. 5.
4. Letter No. 72, 30 April 1811.
5. Letter No. 73, 29 May 1811.
6. Letter No. 62, 9 December 1808.
7. Letter No. 155, 23 March 1817.
8. C. Harman, *Jane's Fame*, Canongate Books, Edinburgh, 2009, p. 66.

JANE'S MAGIC

Jane first went to school aged seven and left just before her eleventh birthday. She returned home and had no further formal education. Not that there was much formality to that she had experienced. She, alongside Cassandra, had been schooled in small private establishments that held little aspiration for their pupils.

Her judgement on what was typical of such schools, and what ought to have been, is given by the narrator of *Emma*:

> 'Mrs. Goddard was the mistress of a school -- not a seminary, or an establishment, or anything which professed, in long sentences of refined nonsense, to combine liberal acquirements with elegant morality, upon new principles and new systems -- and where young ladies for enormous pay might be screwed out of health and into vanity -- but a real, honest, old-fashioned boarding school, where a reasonable quantity of accomplishments were sold at a reasonable price, and where girls might be sent to be out of the way, and scramble themselves into a little education, without any danger of coming back prodigies.' [1]

What competencies would she have acquired by age eleven? Some proficiency in French, music, arithmetic, needlework? Disciplined handwriting. A passion for reading. In her biography of Jane, Claire Tomalin speculates that if Jane may be taken at her own evaluation as a shy child, she would have found refuge from the tribulations of boarding school life in the interior life of reading. [2] From this point (if ever) it seems unlikely that there would have been any planned programme of study; no curriculum, since the prevailing attitudes concerning the education of girls did not favour their being seen as scholars. Indeed, too much learning was regarded as an impediment to their taking their 'natural' domestic place in the world. A sentiment captured with the usual Austen irony in *NA*:

> 'Where people wish to attach, they should always be ignorant. To come with a well-informed mind is to come with an inability of administering to the vanity of others, which a sensible person would always wish to avoid. A woman, especially, if she have the misfortune of knowing anything, should conceal it as well as she can.' [3]

The focus was not on 'learning' in the manner of the true scholar, but rather on 'accomplishments':

> (Mr Darcy, speaking of women who warrant the accolade 'accomplished') 'I cannot boast of knowing more than half-a-dozen, in the whole range of my acquaintance, that are really accomplished...'

> (Miss Bingley) ...'A woman must have a thorough knowledge of music, singing, drawing, dancing, and

the modern languages, to deserve the word; and besides all this, she must possess a certain something in her air and manner of walking, the tone of her voice, her address and expressions, or the word will be but half-deserved.'

'All this she must possess,' added Darcy, 'and to all this she must yet add something more substantial, in the improvement of her mind by extensive reading.'

(Elizabeth Bennet) 'I am no longer surprised at your knowing only six accomplished women. I rather wonder now at your knowing any.' [4]

But whatever the deficiencies in Jane's schooling, it seems the die was cast: her first known works date from this time, and apparently she found her early efforts highly praised, which produced a virtuous cycle with her precocious talent being validated by her family. It seems the learning evident in her writing came from a keen appetite for reading and free access to her father's library, coupled with an encouraging and stimulating home environment; an informal, familial 'book club' with free ranging conversation and exchange of ideas.

There was no 'creative writing course' she could attend. No book on 'The art of the novel'. No model for what was to become her metier. She was evidently a self-starter, and it seems fame was not the spur; she wrote primarily for her own pleasure. Her progress on a subsequent work was not dependent upon the success of an earlier attempt and her books were years in the making. She had four books in-hand before the first was sold (although not published), ten years after she started *Lady Susan* at age seventeen. Early rejection of *First Impressions* (subsequently *P&P*) did not cause her to abandon her craft and she kept faith with her vision throughout her career. There is perhaps more than mere politeness in her refusal of Rev. James Stanier Clarke's (the prince's librarian at Carlton House) importunate suggestions of the direction her work should take than is commonly thought:

> '...But I could no more write a romance than an epic poem. I could not sit seriously down to write a serious romance under any other motive than to save my life; and if it were indispensable for me to keep it up and never relax into laughing at myself or at other people, I am sure I should be hung before I had finished the first chapter. No, I must keep to my own style and go on in my own way; and though I may never succeed again in that, I am convinced that I should totally fail in any other.' [5] (Written in 1816 at age forty.)

Elinor and Marianne (subsequently *S&S*) was drafted in 1795, *First Impressions* in 1796, and it was only in 1797 when Jane was twenty-one that publication was first pursued when her father submitted *First Impressions* to Thomas Cadell, who declined the offer by return of post. She was not chasing quick wins. (See page *ix* for a timeline of all her mature works.)

One of the things that amazes is the maturity of outlook she demonstrates so early in her life. It is one thing to acquire learning but quite another to acquire wisdom. There are few that can extrapolate from a little experience to broad insights about the world (or rather, the people within it - see the quotation from Hume in my introduction).

It is one thing to be precocious in say, mathematics, but that does not require the emotional, empathic experiences and capabilities that underpin maturity. It is possible to be immature and a maths genius. One cannot be immature and a genius writer of novels of manners.

Her juvenilia had a focus on parody which was an inspired choice since it provided a broader target for her to hit; it did not require the same 'fine brush on ivory' of her mature work and allowed her to excel earlier than would otherwise have been the case. Her family would be able to enjoy her work at face value without being obliged to make allowance for her age; genuine unqualified delight and amusement that would do much to fuel Jane's ambition. I do not imagine this was a deliberate conscious choice based on this consideration, I imagine it as simply being the genre that pleased her. And it provided a good foundation for the ironic style she was to develop.

We must distinguish between a love of reading and the urge to write. I believe Jane fell in love with the powerful, and true, magic of language; where the appropriately nuanced incantation may conjure a scene, or a laugh, or give people pause, or a new purpose, or a new direction, or indeed, bend them to your will. She took pleasure in manipulating words, as a sculptor would clay, moulding and reworking them exactly to her purpose. Although she could and did enjoy social occasions, she must have also relished solitude and the opportunity for quiet reflection that the meticulous execution of her craft must have required. Although it was a busy household, for her to produce the drafts of what were to become *S&S* and *P&P*, she must have been able at times to find a secluded space. She must have taken herself off to work in isolation. I can almost hear the cries of, 'Where's Jane?'

We will be forever thankful that, whatever the demerits of the schools Jane attended, they failed to prevent her, as feared by the narrator of *Emma*, from coming back a prodigy.

In his play *The Rivals* (1775) the playwright Sheridan has Sir Anthony Absolute say to Mrs Malaprop, who complains of her independent minded daughter:

> 'It is not to be wonder'd at, Ma'am -- all this is the natural consequence of teaching girls to read. - Had I a thousand daughters, by Heaven! I'd as soon have them taught the black-art [black magic] as their alphabet!' [6]

For Jane, the alphabet was the key to her white magic.

In an entertaining lecture at the Hay Festival in 2014, John Mullan (author of *What Matters in Jane Austen* [7]) considers the number of smiles in *MP*: he reports that there are 74 and that none of them are from Fanny Price! He points out how freighted with significance Henry Crawford's pursuit of Fanny's smile is and that this construction is 'simply' achieved through Jane's cleverness rather than any authorial counting of smiles (which would be a pretty clunky approach and unlikely to yield the desired result). In *P&P,* he reports that there are just twelve smiles from Mr. Darcy and that all but one are for Elizabeth. He points out that, although we might imagine many more from Mr. Wickham, if there were many more from Mr. Darcy he would no longer be 'Mr. Darcy'. The allocation of smiles is a critical consideration.

Mullan also discusses Jane's mastery of 'idiolect'; the provision of a particular 'voice' for each character, wherein each has speech habits that are peculiar to them. He cites Isabella Thorpe's enthusiasm for the adverb 'amazingly' and how this is 'caught' by Catherine; she only uses it after being exposed to Isabella's usage. He de-constructs a variety of Jane's writing in this fashion and provides some fascinating insights into 'how it works'. That is not, however, the same as seeing 'how it was put together'. I originally recoiled from my first thought of comparing the intricate workings to a 'Swiss watch', because of the implication that the mechanism was simply assembled from a set of discrete components, and this would appear to deny the magic that is Jane. But on further reflection I find the analogy to be correct: the 'discrete components' are individual words. It is their intricate interconnectedness that allows the sweep of the hands in synchrony with the heavens – or rather, to abandon that overloaded metaphor, the sweep of the narrative in synchrony with the human condition. Like the best magicians, the act is performed with seamless fluency, but this apparent ease is only achieved through mastery of the technicalities. She was the absolute mistress of nuance; every word is considered in terms of its placement, its tone, its colour, its weight, and how it meshes in a gear train of contextual connotations to produce that magic: *dea ex machina.*[a] Jane had no need to count smiles; her instinctive genius unerringly guided her in the matter of smiles as with everything else.

REFERENCES

1. *Emma*, ch. 3.
2. C. Tomalin, *Jane Austen: A Life*, Penguin Books, 2000, p. 38.
3. *NA*, ch. 14.
4. *P&P*, ch. 8.
5. Letter No. 138(D), 1 April 1816.
6. R. B. Sheridan, *The Rivals: A Comedy*, Project Gutenberg, http://www.gutenberg.org/cache/epub/24761/pg24761-images.html, (date accessed 1.10.2020).
7. J. Mullan, *What Matters in Jane Austen?,* Bloomsbury, London, 2012.

---

[a] *Deus ex machina:* 'God out of the machine' is the more usual expression, but here we have *dea* – 'Goddess'.

JANE'S MANNERS

Jane's books are categorised as 'Novels of Manners', which the Encyclopaedia Britannica defines as, 'works of fiction that re-creates a social world, conveying with finely detailed observation the customs, values, and mores of a highly developed and complex society'. [1]

I do not dispute the accuracy of this categorisation, but it strikes me as a little dry in that it does not relay anything of the dramatic potential or the wit and wisdom that can arise in good quality examples of the type.

There is also perhaps the potential for the uninitiated to regard 'manners' as simply synonymous with etiquette, which would imply a much narrower focus on niceties of formal codes of conduct rather than the very much broader question of human interaction.

Let us nail the popular misapprehension immediately: Jane's books are *not* 'about' courtship, love, marriage, and money. Since you are reading this you will likely not need persuading, but I can perhaps provide some useful ammunition with which you can shoot down this assertion when you encounter it:

Romance, wealth, and standing are just aspects of the environment through which her characters move and engage with one another. Instead, the books are about 'right conduct'; how to behave in consideration of others, act in good faith, and remain true to oneself. And the corresponding fall from grace when failing in this regard, together with the possibility of redemption. (With a side order of social commentary.)

The books are not just civilised, they are civilising. Virginia Woolf understood this:

> 'The wit of Jane Austen has for partner the perfection of her taste. Her fool is a fool, her snob is a snob, because he departs from the model of sanity and sense which she has in mind, and conveys to us unmistakably even while she makes us laugh. Never did any novelist make more use of an impeccable sense of human values. It is against the disc of an unerring heart, an unfailing good taste, an almost stern morality, that she shows up those deviations from kindness, truth, and sincerity which are among the most delightful things in English literature.' [2]

This, most definitely, is not 'chick lit.' But this has not prevented a world of prequels, sequels, and variations from appearing, many of which do warrant that appellation.

One *Pride and Prejudice Intimate Sensual Variation* Amazon Kindle publication took my eye: a book called *Disciplining Miss Bennet* by Vivienne Norville. I approached with trepidation. I quote verbatim from the Amazon listing page as it stood as of July 2020:

> '*Disciplining Miss Bennet* is part 1 of a sensual and steamy Pride and Prejudice variation that grows in heat throughout the series. This short story features a spanking scene and following iterations are best enjoyed by readers over 18 years of age.' [3]

'Miss Bennet': so, it seems it is Jane (the eldest Bennet daughter) that is being disciplined? (Not Miss Elizabeth Bennet.)[a] 'Grows in heat' rather than 'gets hotter'? Following iterations? What of the current one? 'Best enjoyed' – meaning 'preferred by' or 'recommended for' those aged over eighteen?

An inauspicious beginning: nevertheless, being over 18, I took the plunge (purely in the interests of research you understand). I find I cannot recommend the book. It is not so much 'fine brush on ivory' as 'broad pasting-brush on billboard'.

Spoiler alert: the spanker and 'spankee' are not, as you might have imagined, Lady Catherine de Bourgh and Mr Collins.

The Amazon page goes on to advertise, '*Disciplining Miss Bennet* is Part 1 of 3 in the "*Taken In Hand By Mr. Darcy*" series

---

[a] The eldest unmarried daughter would be known as Miss Bennet (without the use of her Christian name), younger unmarried daughters as Miss Elizabeth Bennet, Miss Mary Bennet etc.

of short story serials.' [4]

I will not be exploring Parts Two and Three (I could not stand any more heat). My first thought was that Jane would be appalled, but on second thought, I suspect she would have been amused.

REFERENCES

1. Encyclopaedia Britannica,
https://www.britannica.com/art/novel-of-manners, (date accessed 3.10.2020).
2. V.Woolf, *The Common Reader*, (e-book) Green Light, Los Angeles 2012,
3. V. Norville, *Disciplining Miss Bennet*, Vivienne Norville, 2020, Amazon Kindle, accessed July 2020.
4. *Ibid.*

4

INTERLUDE - JANE'S LIES

It is one of the most celebrated sentences in all English literature, and is characteristically, almost definitively, 'Jane'. The intriguing thing is that it boldly asserts three propositions that are all untrue!

'It is a truth *[not true]*, universally acknowledged *[not true]*, that a single man in possession of a good fortune, must *[not true]* be in want of a wife.' [1]

And yet, despite all the falsehoods, there is truth here! It is a truth that is recognised although artfully hidden behind hyperbole and misdirection. The simple truth is that it is widely recognised that a rich single man will be an attractive marriage prospect for many women. This truth is so 'universally acknowledged', that baldly stated in this manner it is a banality. And yet from this sow's ear, Jane fashions the most wonderful silk purse. It is the 'lies' that allow this. The transformation is handled by recruiting us as co-conspirators so that we may congratulate ourselves on our insight. The particular twist that delights is the reversal of 'want' from those attracted by the eligibility of the single man, to the man himself.

It may well be that the 'single man' may be in want of a wife, but that is not because of his fortune; it would perhaps be for want of an heir or social position, whereas a single man with a fortune will be wanted simply by virtue of that fortune. It should be 'universally acknowledged' that this was and remains true of a single woman in possession of a fortune. But interestingly, the corresponding formulation does not work:

It is a truth, universally acknowledged, that a single **woman** *in possession of a good fortune, must be in want of a* **husband**.

There is something almost distasteful about this: it lacks all charm, it does not prompt a smile, it does not lift our mood in the manner of the original. Why should this be when it is the exact female gender equivalent?

I believe it is because it lacks the implicit gallantry of the original. It may be unfair, and entirely 'politically incorrect', but I suspect there is a widespread (if not universal) 'acknowledgement' that many single women, regardless of fortune, will be in want of a husband. This view would not be at all controversial in the early 19th century and might well have been regarded as 'universal'. However, although understood, it would not be gallant to openly acknowledge this want, or more particularly, to impute its presence in any individual woman. Women could not actively declare or act upon their 'want' other than to do what they could to present opportunities for men to meet with them and seek their company.

'Undoubtedly, there is meanness in all the arts which ladies sometimes condescend to employ for captivation. Whatever bears affinity to cunning is despicable.' - Mr Darcy (well, Jane actually!) [2]

The initiative lay with the man and it was only when his intentions were clearly established as honourable, and there could be no doubt of his sincerity, that a lady might acknowledge any reciprocal feelings.

The original formulation observes this nicety by displacing the declaration of want to the man, and this is boldly asserted – although immediately understood to really be with the woman – which is the entire joke. The second formulation offends because it does not observe this gallantry and ends up striking a sour, churlish note, because the untruth in 'must' is this time so much less profound – it is so much less of a lie, the general expectation being that a woman would indeed want a husband. (However, as a matter of logic it remains a lie because 'must' allows no exceptions.)

There is an implicit romanticism in the original that is absent in its sister. The wilful misrepresentation in the original is cynical, yes, but the cynicism is gracefully expressed with wit and charm.

REFERENCES

1. *P&P*, ch. 1 (Line 1!).
2. *P&P*, ch. 8.

THE STING IN THE ENTAIL

It is feature of some of Jane's works that they explicitly make dramatic use of the dependence of unmarried daughters on the continuing charity of their father or brother(s): we have the Bennet girls exposed through the entail on Longbourn (the legal stipulation that means Mr Collins, as the closest male relation, stands to inherit the property), and more particularly for my current purpose, we have the Dashwood sisters obliged to leave their home and reliant upon the benevolence of their brother, John, because of the legal constraints placed upon their father through his inheritance.

These stories were shared with the family long before their eventual publication. Did her father and brothers squirm as they heard of the Dashwood family's plight? Her father certainly was not prompted to make any provision for Jane or Cassandra; his will was written (in 1770) before they were born, and he left them nothing. He left everything to his wife.[a]

---

[a] In addition to the previous examples of unmarried daughters in Jane's novels, there is also the pathos of Miss Bates, but she

We do not have any evidence of any ill feeling being generated by this story, no angry reactions about being 'lectured' by an ungrateful daughter/sister. Jane's father is known to have been supportive and encouraging. He gave her the gift of the portable writing desk and went so far as to attempt to secure publication of *First Impressions* (the precursor to *P&P*) on Jane's behalf.

How can this be? To write as she did of the plight of the Dashwood sisters seems so very pointed: the parallels, should Elinor and Marianne not marry, with Jane's circumstances seem so close that there could be no mistaking them. We must be mindful that the 'absence of evidence is not proof of absence' and it is conceivable that evidence of any upset or argument has been tactfully left out of the record, but it strikes me that Jane would not want to be found wilfully disobliging toward her father or her brothers, and had there been any upset she would not have persisted with the plot device. It seems to me more likely that there was no ill feeling arising because there was no perception of being 'lectured' and indeed, no lecturing intent.

I imagine that amongst a close family such as the Austen's, the expectation of fraternal support was so innate that there was simply no ground upon which a seed of doubt might germinate. And at that time, management of business affairs was almost exclusively the prerogative of the men. (That said, it is notable that when her brother Henry fell ill, Jane undertook direct negotiations with her publisher, John

---

cannot be called as a witness for the prosecution since Emma was written long after Jane's father died.

Murray: 'He is a rogue of course, but a civil one'. [1]) We should remember that until the *Married Women's Property Acts of 1870* and *1882*, upon marriage a woman lost all control of her property and income; perhaps there was a wish to avoid the possibility of such dissipation? Interestingly this was true of copyright also: had she married; any copyright Jane held would have become her husband's.

If that was the thinking behind the absence of any inheritance, it must be said that the manoeuvre failed: with Henry's bankruptcy in 1816 there most certainly was dissipation. Jane herself lost £13 – not a trivial sum to her by any means, and Henry and Frank were no longer able to continue the annual £50 contribution they had each previously made to their mother's household. Henry's uncle Leigh-Perrot lost £10,000, and his brother Edward £20,000. Consider here the continuing absence of evidence of ill-feeling. Claire Tomalin says of the episode, 'Austen accounts of Henry's crash are reticent'. [2] The few references speak of misfortune rather than blame. It is difficult to imagine that there were not some acrimonious exchanges in the immediate aftermath of the cataclysm even if family loyalties allowed a retrospective philosophical view to emerge.

In *Eavesdropping on Jane Austen's England*, authors Roy and Lesley Adkins cite William Hayley as saying, of an unmarried woman from a good family,

> 'It is probable, that after having passed the sprightly years of youth in the comfortable mansion of an opulent father, she is reduced to the shelter of some contracted lodging in a country town, attended by a

single female servant, and with difficulty living on the interest of two or three thousand pounds, reluctantly, and perhaps irregularly, paid to her by an avaricious or extravagant brother, who considers such payment as a heavy incumbrance on his paternal estate. Such is the condition in which the unmarried daughters of English gentlemen are too frequently found.' [3]

Perhaps within the Austen family, it was unthinkable that the brothers would neglect their sisters. And yet it was entirely thinkable of other families.

REFERENCES

1. Letter No. 121, 17 October 1815.
2. C. Tomalin, *Jane Austen; A Life,* Penguin Books, 2000, p. 258.
3. R & L. Adkins, *Eavesdropping on Jane Austen's England*, Abacus, 2014, p. 15.

6

THE TROUBLE WITH TOM

It seems that it is popularly accepted as fact that Jane was in love with Tom Lefroy; an idea promoted by the 2007 film *Becoming Jane*. [1] We have a reported admission of 'boyish love' much later in Tom's life. [2] (His liaison with Jane took place when they were both twenty.) There is no known reciprocal admission from Jane; there are only the somewhat cryptic observations in three letters to Cassandra. There is woefully little to go on.

Were these the only letters that included references to Tom? Were there others that included potentially hurtful or embarrassing references to him, or that were destroyed for other reasons? If the 'affair', if we may call it that, was in any way an embarrassment, and such embarrassment was a basis of selection for destruction, why would Cassandra preserve any letters that made mention of it?

Clearly there was a relationship between Jane and Tom and something more than mere acquaintance. That relationship was known to Cassandra. But the tone is satirical, mocking even.

Mockery of Tom? Of Jane herself? Of the two of them? Is this tone a matter of self-defence against burgeoning feelings that had no prospect of fulfilment? Or is it not in fact dissembling, but a straightforward expression of amusement?

Tom Lefroy's nephew (T. E. P. Lefroy) reported that towards the end of his life his uncle admitted to a 'boyish love'. Perhaps we should take this at face value and understand that his love really was 'boyish' and was perceived to be so by Jane; something presenting charm and amusement but not in any way threatening in terms of Jane's self-possession or equilibrium. On the other hand, I wonder how else a man in his nineties might be expected to characterise a relationship from his twenties?

If we accept that there were no secrets between Jane and Cassandra, why is not there more for us to draw on here. Was there more in the way of 'juicy' revelation that has been excised? My instinct is that we are denied nothing of substance in this matter. If this were a real affair of the heart, I believe there would have been frank declarations alongside the mockery. An admission of real feeling coupled with the defensive mockery to assure Cassandra (and perhaps Jane herself) that there was no real emotional peril. Jane reports the idea of being separated as 'melancholy' rather than as devastating; she does not report that she is prostrate with grief.

There is her curious declaration that,

> 'l rather expect to receive an offer from my friend in the course of the evening, I shall refuse him, however, unless he promises to give away his white Coat'.ᵃ [3]

Was this a real expectation? If so, it is difficult to interpret the mocking dismissive tone other than as reflecting Jane's own assessment of Tom's love as 'boyish' and not worthy of serious consideration. She says, 'rather expect', not 'hope for' or 'have reason to expect'; there is no equivocation. It has been suggested that the offer was of a dance rather than marriage, but would a gentleman 'offer' a dance or 'request' one? The meaning must have been clear to Cassandra; it is difficult to imagine Jane would be deliberately ambiguous on such a point. If Jane did indeed have any expectation of an offer of marriage it is difficult to imagine she would be quite so flippant, for that would imply a degree of contempt inconsistent with enjoyment of Tom's company in terms of 'sitting down together'.

It seems that Tom was dismissed to London by his aunt (Mrs Lefroy), 'because he had behaved so ill to Jane', as her son reported, and 'so that no more mischief might be done'. [4]

The one aspect of the letters that suggests more substantial emotional engagement from Jane is her report to Cassandra that,

> 'At length the day is come on which I am to flirt my

ᵃ Jane makes fun of Tom Lefroy's 'white coat', understood to be a reference to the eponymous hero in Fielding's novel *The Adventures of Tom Jones.*

last with Tom Lefroy, and when you receive this it will be over. My tears flow as I write at the melancholy idea. Wm. Chute called here yesterday...'.
[5]

This does not appear to carry the same mockery; possibly Jane's expectation was that the mockery would be understood as a given from the established context.

Possible perhaps, but I am not persuaded. The other strange thing is the abrupt transition to the report of Wm. Chute's visit; there is no qualification of the upset, no reassurance that it was a transient episode only. Was the sharpness of the transition intended to give the lie to the previous declaration and therein lies the mockery?

In another letter to Cassandra in 1798, nearly three years after the liaison, Jane declares herself too proud to make any enquiries on meeting with Tom's aunt:

> 'Mrs. Lefroy did come last Wednesday, and the Harwoods came likewise, but very considerately paid their visit before Mrs. Lefroy's arrival, with whom, in spite of interruptions both from my father and James, I was enough alone to hear all that was interesting, which you will easily credit when I tell you that of her nephew she said nothing at all, and of her friend (Revd Samuel Blackall – another potential suitor) very little. She did not once mention the name of the former to <u>me</u>, and I was too proud to make any enquiries; but on my father's afterwards asking where he was, I learnt that he was gone back to London in his way to Ireland, where he is called

to the Bar and means to practise.' [6]

I find this to be the more telling record. I cannot believe it beyond Jane's skill to frame an enquiry in a manner that would avoid humiliation. And this is nearly three years later! Mrs Lefroy was a close friend who resided nearby at Ashe Rectory; there would have been intermediate opportunities to enquire about Tom. It seems the particular difficulty arose because Tom stayed at Ashe that autumn, but did not visit Steventon, and did not meet with Jane; instead he became 'the elephant in the room'. The implication is that the meeting with Mrs Lefroy was the first opportunity for enquiry *after* Tom's stay. And yet we might anticipate that *not* to enquire about Tom would appear pointed and invite just as much notice. Certainly, one explanation of Jane's reticence is that she had an acute sensitivity here. We might speculate that she did not want to discomfort her friend by referencing an awkward episode, but why then 'too proud' rather than 'too concerned' (of giving hurt)? Possibly Jane considered Mrs Lefroy's original dismissal of Tom to be an unwarranted interference? And if wanting to reassure that no real damage was done, why not enquire in an unconcerned manner that demonstrated this? Could it be that Jane was sufficiently disobliged by her friend's historical interference to not want to give her the satisfaction of demonstrating an interest that might be perceived as confirming the interference justified; it might then remain a dormant point of contention.

Mrs Lefroy was a close friend, but that is not to say they were intimate in the manner of Jane and her sister (who 'had not a thought concealed from her'). They were separated by a generation.

I have a sense that Jane would not write to her confidante sister in such a flippant manner if Tom had been a serious contender for Jane's heart or hand. My assessment of the balance of probabilities is that there was a dalliance that Jane enjoyed, but nothing beyond that. Jane could have said, as Emma does of Frank Churchill, 'He has imposed on me, but he has not injured me'. [7] It being the imposition that Mrs Lefroy saw and acted to curtail.

REFERENCES

1. J. Jarrold, et. al., *Becoming Jane*, Alliance Films, Montreal, 2007.
2. Cited in C. Tomalin, *Jane Austen: A Life*, Penguin Books, London, 2000, p. 120
3. Letter No. 2, 14 January 1796.
4. Cited in C. Tomalin, *Jane Austen: A Life*, Penguin Books, London, 2000, p. 120.
5. Letter No. 2, 14 January 1796.
6. Letter No. 11, 17 November 1798.
7. *Emma,* ch. 49.

7

JANE'S LOVE LIFE

For a woman in Jane's position as one of the gentry, the societal costs, the 'fallout' associated with a pregnancy outside of marriage, make it practically certain that she would have remained celibate throughout her life. To risk a liaison would have been an act of madness and the obstacles of social conventions regarding unaccompanied women and the likelihood of indiscreet behaviour being observed by servants would mean that there was little prospect of a spontaneous act of passion; it would have required premeditation and a degree of planning with a wilful disregard for the risks.

Her writing shows that she understood the nature of sexual passion and its influence on male-female relations. There is of course the sexual undercurrent in the nascent relationships between her protagonists: Elizabeth and Darcy, Emma and Knightley, Anne and Captain Wentworth, Marianne and Willoughby, but curiously not Fanny and Edmund? These aspects are not explicitly declared or explored in her books and, to my mind, so much the better for it. That is not to say that such explorations cannot be well executed (although notoriously difficult), but such explorations belong to a different genre altogether. Some readers are frustrated by this omission; they have a yearning to explore the physicality of the implicit passion and sexual tension, and some authors have attempted to fill the 'gap' with reworkings of the stories in a modern setting. I understand the motivation but cannot help but feel a sense of betrayal on Jane's behalf. Write your own story! For many it is the implicit nature of the passion that lends Jane's romances particular power. There can be a latent force in a look or the touch of hands that cannot be matched by any overt act of intimacy. To travel hopefully is a better thing than to arrive…

Charlotte Brontë famously wrote of Jane,

> '…the Passions are perfectly unknown to her; she rejects even a speaking acquaintance with that stormy sisterhood'… [1]

But this is nonsense; a consistent theme in Jane's work is the need to govern the passions, to check unbridled sensibility. (This particular extract from Charlotte's letter is known to many Janeites, but much less so the letter from which it is drawn; see 'Appendix 1 - Charlotte's Letters'.)

There are several references to reckless abandonment of sexual restraint and the consequences that ensue, for example:

In *S&S* we have the seduction and abandonment by Willoughby of a young girl.

In *P&P* we have Lydia's elopement with Wickham.

In *MP* there is Maria Bertram's adultery and Julia Bertram's elopement.

There is however nothing to suggest she had a corresponding understanding of homosexual attraction; she did not explore or exploit this in any of her novels. But this is to be expected given the social codes of her day; absence of evidence is here not necessarily evidence of absence.

It is likely Jane would have understood something of the physical 'mechanics' of a sexual relationship; she was raised in the country after all. And she may well have been further educated through conversation with her more experienced and somewhat racy cousin, Eliza de Feuillide.

There is every indication that Jane did find men attractive and that she enjoyed the flirtations and the relatively (for the time) intimate interactions at social functions such as balls. Such attraction is of course the precursor to greater intimacy and ultimately the prospect of a full sexual relationship. In that respect, Jane may be said to have explored these precursors, even if she did not pursue them to their potential conclusion.[a]

And, forgive the indelicacy, some solo exploration would have given her some insight to the associated sensations. In common with the rest of humanity she would have extrapolated in her imagination from these beginnings to an expectation of the full act. But whatever the pleasures associated with sexual congress; it is only rendered uplifting by mutual affection; considered dispassionately or merely as a matter of self-gratification, the physical act, the 'beast with two backs', remains ridiculous and more fitting for the

---

[a] I was tempted to write 'potential climax(!)' but my editor's better judgement prevailed.

farmyard. I am persuaded that Jane understood this. For all we know, she may have lusted, but for Jane, without love there was no aspiration for marriage, and without marriage there was no prospect of consummation. The absence of any such prospect does not mean that the initial attraction phase cannot remain pleasurable; it can be an end in itself; the thrill really can be in the chase.

REFERENCES

1. Letter from Charlotte Brontë to William Smith Williams, 12 April 1850 in J. Barker, *The Brontës: A Life in Letters*, Little, Brown, London, 2016.

JANE'S PROPOSAL

So, what might we infer from Jane's retraction of her acceptance of Harris Bigg-Wither's marriage proposal?

A remarkable episode. One, if we take her sensibilities as granted, that must have been truly distressing to Jane.

To recount the circumstances, which were relayed at second-hand by Caroline, (daughter of Mary Austen and Jane's brother James) from her mother's recollection:[a] Jane and her sister, Cassandra, had left Bath to stay with James and Mary, who now had possession of the Steventon Rectory. They left Steventon to stay with their long-established and well-to-do family friends at Manydown Park, some four miles from Steventon, and home to the Bigg-Wither family, including sisters Alethea and Catherine and their brother Harris.

On the evening of 2nd December 1802 Jane accepted a proposal of marriage from Harris and we may imagine the celebratory mood of the party and the many expressions of felicitation (each a metaphorical hammer blow on the nails

---

[a] And perhaps should not, therefore, be taken for established fact as it is usually is?

of Jane's literary coffin?).

However, the following morning Jane retracted her acceptance. Under the circumstances, it is understandable that Jane and Cassandra immediately left Manydown Park to avoid any further awkwardness for all concerned. (But might this also be true if there were no acceptance and just a rejection?) Relations were not severed however; quite a testament to the solid foundations of friendship between the families.

There is no direct witness testimony available from any of those present at Manydown Park that December; is this a telling gap that underlines the pain and embarrassment arising or has the incident been (perhaps inadvertently) misrepresented? For present purposes I take the reported circumstances at face value.

The fact of the retraction within 24 hours suggests that Jane had not previously considered the possibility of a proposal from Harris; had not beforehand subjected the notion to a comprehensive 'cost-benefit analysis'. (Unromantic terminology, but appropriate nevertheless.) It seems he must have caught her off guard? There must then have been no previous indications of 'warm regard'? No knowing remarks from family or friends? Given a surprise proposal, the obvious thing to do would be to ask for time to consider, but no, Jane accepts! I think we may reasonably infer the influence of drink; a heady mix of alcohol, high spirits and a party atmosphere. Jane drunk! This may not fit with notions of Jane's infallible propriety (which for many, together with her wit, is her defining characteristic) but it is an altogether human possibility. I submit that it offers a simple, plausible explanation for her actions.

We can only imagine Jane's torture that night; the agonies she must have undergone as she retrospectively undertook the 'cost-benefit analysis'. And the result; the mortifying retraction in full realisation of the injury she must inflict on Harris and that she would inflict on herself. The disappointment. She did not at that late stage ask for time to consider, which might have been a possible 'manoeuvre' to take some of the immediate sting out of the interview, and perhaps through delay to soften the ultimate blow of rejection? On the other hand, any delay would give others the opportunity to bring arguments to bear in favour of continuing with the marriage, arguments that Jane did not want to hear at that point?

Having made up her mind, it was clear that an immediate unequivocal retraction was the only proper course. But it is one thing to recognise the proper thing to do and quite another to act upon it when this may add to personal discomfiture, particularly when already suffering stress and confusion. In that respect we may see the immediate retraction as a courageous act.

The 'benefit' of the proposal is clear: financial security and mistress of her own house; security also, at one remove so to speak, for Cassandra. For Jane to have been persuaded to retraction, the 'costs' must be correspondingly high.

From several well-known remarks in her novels you might think Jane would have been anxious to marry:

> 'Single women have a dreadful propensity for being poor. Which is one very strong argument in favour of matrimony.' (Letter from Jane to her niece Fanny.) [1]

> '...it was the only honourable provision for well-educated young women of small fortune, and however uncertain of giving happiness, must be their pleasantest preservative from want.' (Narrator in *Pride and Prejudice* speaking of marriage.) [2]

> 'A single woman with a very narrow income must be a ridiculous, disagreeable old maid - the proper sport of boys and girls.' (Emma speaking to Harriet in *Emma* [3] and we have the figure of Miss Bates as a further warning.)

Given that she herself had a distinctly narrow income and faced the very real prospect of becoming an 'old maid', why did she not marry?

There are of course other remarks that contradict the sentiments expressed above:

> 'Anything is to be preferred or endured rather than marrying without affection.' (Jane in a letter to her niece Fanny.) [4]

> 'Nothing is to be compared to the misery of being bound without Love, bound to one, & preferring another. That is a Punishment which you do not deserve.' (Jane in a letter to her niece Fanny.) [5]

> 'Oh, Lizzy! do anything rather than marry without

affection.' (Jane Bennet in *Pride and Prejudice*.) [6]

It is perhaps in Charlotte Lucas (from *P&P*) that we have the finest advocate in refuting this last counsel. Charlotte, who has sense and sensibility enough for Elizabeth to find her a particular friend, but who nevertheless knowingly contracts marriage with a man she knows to be ridiculous. Mr Collins may be inept and unwittingly boorish, but he is not evil, and we must assume that Charlotte has talent enough to train him and have him come to heel. Surely her acceptance must be because she has seen he is pliable and biddable.

And it is, of course, in the competing demands of sense and sensibility that the roots of the contradictory statement above may be found.

Jane has here rehearsed the arguments in favour of a marriage without affection; and they found sufficient force to prompt her to initially accept Bigg-Wither's proposal. And we should perhaps distinguish between absence of affection and absence of 'true love'.

It is when sense and sensibility are in proper alignment that her heroines find fulfilment; in each of her major novels the journey is towards this alignment. In persuading Anne Elliott against betrothal to Captain Wentworth,[b] Lady Russell cannot have argued want of sensibility, it must have been want of sense, and once this impediment is removed we have alignment and fulfilment.

---

[b] In Jane's novel, *Persuasion*.

So, why in the end did Jane not marry?

When Cassandra's fiancé died, it may be that Cassandra determined not to marry and given the bond between Jane and Cassandra, we may speculate that Jane decided to share Cassandra's fate in that regard. Certainly, the relationship between the sisters was to have been changed by Cassandra's marriage, but there was perhaps then the expectation that both would marry. That would no longer be true if Cassandra determined on remaining single. It is tempting to see sisterly devotion as a consideration here, but if Jane had married Bigg-Wither she would have had the wealth and position to provide security for both Cassandra and her mother. Sisterly devotion would find new resources, and, on these grounds, I think we may dismiss the idea as being a dominant consideration.

In terms of balancing costs, Jane must certainly have identified the dangers of childbirth, but if this had been a particular fear of hers it would seem unlikely that she would ever have considered marriage. More telling I suspect, given her temperament and talent, would be the loss of the independent agency that provided the fulfilment she found through writing. The 'life of the mind' that she enjoyed was not especially demanding of wealth, but it did require freedom from the concerns that the mistress of a household and growing brood would be subject to; even if the time could be found, the 'mental space' likely could not. It seems likely the unacceptable price was the loss of this agency; not an absolute loss, since she would have new resources with which to exercise her will, but not perhaps in directions that interested her – I suspect she feared she would have lost her true self. Possibly she might have been reconciled to this loss if sense and sensibility had found alignment in a Mr Darcy/Knightley, but in their absence it was a compromise too far.

Harris was 21, Jane 27. He had not completed his studies at Worcester College, Oxford and is reported as being tall, plain, and socially awkward, at least in part due to a stammer. From these reports, although presumably not finding him objectionable, it seems unlikely that Jane would even have found his demeanour merely 'pleasing'; it is inconceivable that she would find his company thrilling. What if the proposal had come from an intelligent, articulate, attractive suitor? A 'Tom Lefroy' in all but name? (Perhaps even wearing a dark coat!ᶜ) What then would have been the outcome? I believe there would have been no retraction. Since things were sufficiently in the balance for Jane to make an immediately regretted acceptance, we can deduce that it would not take much to tip things in favour of continuance. This might well, of course, have led to repentance at leisure.

Did Jane's experience with this proposal inform her writing? Not in any direct way it seems; there is no acceptance-retraction episode in her novels, although the dramatic potential is clear. Perhaps to attempt to use it would have been too uncomfortable in resurrecting the memories? Possibly it would have been considered an impropriety in referencing an episode, of her making, that was painful to others she was close to. It would certainly constitute 'life

---

ᶜ In a letter to Cassandra, Jane makes fun of Tom Lefroy's 'white coat', understood to be a reference to Fielding's novel '*The Adventures of Tom Jones*'.

experience' and may well have fuelled her imagination in her exposition of such marriage proposals as do arise. Although drafts of *P&P*, *S&S* and *NA* predate Bigg-Wither's proposal, they all have extended gestation periods that bracket the episode and it is possible that revisions were made to the proposal scenes in the light of her experience. Certainly, her pen offers many contributions to each side of the balance, including the 'dreadful propensity' for single women to be poor and the admonition to 'do anything rather than marry without affection.'

REFERENCES

1. Letter No. 153, 13 March 1817.
2. *P&P*, ch. 22.
3. *Emma*, ch. 10.
4. Letter No.114, 30 November 1814.
5. *Ibid.*
6. *P&P*, ch. 59.

9

JANE'S MARRIAGE

Before Lord Hardwicke's *Marriage Act of 1754*, it was possible for couples to elope and marry clandestinely, the only mandatory requirement for a valid marriage being that it be celebrated by an Anglican clergyman.

The act meant that, to be valid, there had to be publication of banns (proclamations) and celebration in a parish church of one of the marriage party, or the issue of a licence. A licence would allow an earlier wedding since it dispensed with the need for the banns to be published for three Sundays prior to the wedding, and it would allow the marriage to take place other than in a home parish. The licence and banns were introduced as mechanisms intended to prevent marriages where there was some impediment, for example, absence of consent, a prohibited degree of kinship, or a pre-existing marriage.

To circumvent the act, eloping couples could travel to Scotland and it is for this reason that Gretna Green (just over the border with England) became associated with runaway couples.

Both the banns and marriages were recorded in the Parish Register. A 1754 register book publication for this purpose carried an example of the required entry format on the reverse of the title page. It is on such an exemplar that Jane's 'marriage' is recorded. This graffito by Jane is relatively faint and not suitable for reproduction here (images may be found on-line). Difficulties are compounded by the show through of the printed title from the other side of the page, which also carries a further graffito.

To facilitate matters I transcribe the text as shown on the next pages. This is not a facsimile, I take some small liberties here with layout and style, but this remains a largely faithful representation in these respects. (The 'copperplate' script and struck through text represents Jane's hand.)

THE

REGISTER-BOOK *of the Parish*

of Steventon For the Registering of all *in the County of South Hampton*

BANNS and MARRIAGES,

Published or solemnised

In the Parish-Church of the Parish of

Steventon in the County of South Hampton

The Form of an Entry of Publication of Banns

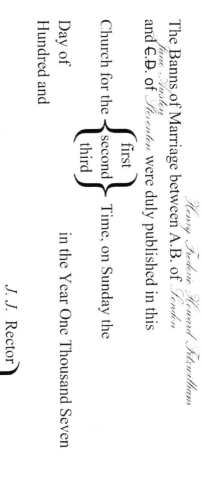

The Banns of Marriage between A.B. of *Jane Austen* and C.D. of *December* were duly published in this

Henry Frederic Howard Fitzwilliam of London

Church for the { first / second / third } Time, on Sunday the

Day of

Hundred and

in the Year One Thousand Seven

J. J. Rector
Vicar
Curate

The Form of an Entry of a Marriage

Edmund Arthur William Mortimer *Jane Austen*

A.B. of *Liverpool* and C.D. of *Steventon*

Were married in this Church by { Banns | Licence* } this

in the Year One Thousand Seven

Day of

Hundred and by me

J. J. Rector | Vicar | Curate

This Marriage was solemnized between us A.B. C.B. late C.D. *Jack Smith and Jane Smith late Austen*

In the Presence of E.F.G.H. *Jack Smith, Jane Smith* *Jack Smith, Jane Smith*

A number of things are notable to my mind. The incompleteness of the record is a surprise; my expectation was of a diligently made simulation of a true record. And it is not as though Jane was interrupted; she went on to make an entry of the banns or the marriage before completing whichever she made first. It seems it was the naming of the parties was the component that fascinated her rather than the niceties of the record itself.

The two entries are not consistent of course, being for different grooms. And Jane makes a mistake(!): the placeholder characters 'A.B., C.D.' etc. show that the couple's names are to be repeated, including the bride's maiden name, where they sign to testify to the solemnisation. (The prior entry being made by the clergyman.) It seems Jane thought this testimony was to be made by the witnesses, who are recorded separately in lieu of 'E.F. G.H.'.

The significance, if any, of the chosen names eludes me, although the repetition through the initials H.F.H.F. suggests some deliberate scheme. There is no obvious link to her brothers' names. (James, George, Edward, Henry Thomas, Francis William (Frank), Charles John.)

On the title page, given the entry in the designated space for the parish, the addition above appears redundant. It might be thought one thing to write on the model entry but quite another to deface the title page of an official register that was under the guardianship of her father. But then why was this left blank in the first place allowing Jane the opportunity?

In *The Spirituality of Jane Austen*, the authoress Paula Hollingsworth sees the entries as, 'One touching proof of

Revd George Austen's indulgence of his younger daughter's childish imagination…' [1] which may be the case. On the other hand, he may have taken a dim view of Jane's defacing of church property. If he had supervised the entry, he might have been expected to prevent the mistakes? Certainly, this was a considered act; there were no pocket pens allowing a spontaneous entry on a moment's whim.

The original shows a hand that appears relatively refined and mature; this is no childish scrawl. The reports of this graffito ascribe it to her teenage years. I am uncertain on what basis, presumably from a comparison with her handwriting from dated manuscripts? But if she were a teenager, I have difficulty imagining her to be much more than the first candidate age of thirteen. I speculate that if Jane were more mature than this, she would be embarrassed to be discovered indulging in such fantasies.

REFERENCES

1. P. Hollingsworth, *The Spirituality of Jane Austen*, Lion Books, Oxford, 2017, p. 28.

10

JANE'S DARK SIDE

There are any number of 'mean girls' in Jane's work, but only one that could be properly characterised as a *femme fatale*:

Lucy Steele is described by Elinor Dashwood as '…illiterate, artful and selfish' [1] but possesses low cunning rather than sophistication.

Lydia Bennet may be wilful, impulsive, and inconsiderate of others, '…a determined flirt', [2] but she is also naïve and transparent and with no idea of how to play a long game.

Isabella Thorpe is beautiful and calculating but lacks depth: 'She is a vain coquette, and her tricks have not answered.' [3]

Mary Crawford of *Mansfield Park* might be considered a candidate, but I find her candidacy is largely due to what she does *not* do rather than what she does; her sins are of omission rather than commission. She fails to censure morally dubious behaviour in others. Certainly, she might damage men within her orbit, but that would perhaps be inadvertent collateral damage rather than her outright intent. There may be a parallel with the crime of manslaughter as distinct from murder; the outcome is the same, but the latter requires 'malice aforethought', whereas the former is unintentional. Her philosophy might be expressed as, 'All being fair in love and war'. I do not find she qualifies.

We may distinguish between the *coquette* and the true *femme fatale*, who wilfully entices men to their downfall: the *coquette* charms without sincerity to gain the attention and admiration of men but does not purposefully inflict harm. Any harm would be inadvertent and typically limited to distraction rather than destruction. More *dérangeant* than *fatale*.

With the *femme fatale*, the obvious metaphor to reach for is that of a 'moth to a flame', but that would be an injustice to moths; moths believe the light to be that of the moon and do not recognise the danger. Men, being stupider, perceive the hazard of the 'flame' but seek to engage with it anyway.

It is in *Lady Susan* we find a woman who could bring men to their doom, very much with malice aforethought, and who would, without compunction, use men for sport, particularly if they have slighted her, or attempted to thwart her designs.

It has been conjectured that Mary Crawford is a development of Lady Susan who is herself modelled on Eliza de Feuillide, the vivacious cousin and self-confessed flirt who eventually married Jane's brother Henry. It is a plausible hypothesis, but once you start looking for such connections it is inevitable that they will be found, somewhat in the nature of 'ley lines' (straight line alignments between landmarks and historic structures, which will, in a sufficiently populated environment, arise by chance and not hold any significance). Jane's works were noted for their 'true to life' quality that distinguished them from the romantic and fantastical that were the usual fare to be found in novels of her day. It should be no surprise then that similarities should be found between the characters in her books and persons known to her, since, being actual living beings, they would have exhibited 'true to life' characteristics! Of course, her experiences with people would inform her authentic characterisation; how could it be otherwise? But there is a world of difference between being 'informed by' and 'modelled on'. To introduce a character explicitly based on a friend or acquaintance would, I speculate, have been seen by Jane as a gross impertinence. Other parallels beside that of Lady Susan/Eliza have been postulated but given these considerations I believe all such 'nuggets' to be 'fool's gold'. The interested reader will likely enjoy the discussion in the Appendix to *Jane Austen's Literary Manuscripts*. [4]

I have the impression that Jane relished her creation of Lady Susan: there is no censorious tone; the tone is rather one of admiration for a woman who outmanoeuvres men and uses her 'womanly wiles' as a fitting response to the tyranny of a patriarchal world. It may be that *Lady Susan* is closer to the parodies of Jane's youthful works, since it is believed to have been begun when she was just seventeen, but she is also believed to have been still developing the work at age thirty. Unless it was very extensively developed, the work demonstrates profound insight for a teenager. This itself has led to speculation that the characterisation must be due to reproduction rather than invention. In her book *Personal Aspects of Jane Austen,* Miss Mary Augusta Austen-Leigh writes, 'Critics have observed, not unnaturally, that this remarkable analysis of a vicious woman's nature seems a strange subject for a young girl either to have attempted or to have succeeded in…' Austen-Leigh goes on to conclude that,

> 'She could not have depicted an inhuman, repulsive mother, carrying on her barbarities beneath a mask of charm and beauty, without having constantly before her thoughts the prototype of this exceptional character, of whose actual existence she was well aware.' [5]

(The prototype referred to is a Mrs Craven, whose granddaughters were friends of Jane and from whom it is speculated she could have heard of the depravations of their grandmother. To my mind, a character based on such third-hand reports would be 'inspired by' rather than 'modelled on'.) Given the juvenile parodies, I see no reason to see the subject as a strange one 'to have attempted'; we can agree on its being 'strange' to 'have succeeded in', but such 'strangeness' is to be expected from a literary genius.

In *Jane Austen, Her Life and Letters*, the authors write of *Lady Susan*:

> 'There is hardly any attempt at a plot, or at the grouping of various characters; such as exist are kept in the background, and serve chiefly to bring into bolder relief the one full-length, highly finished, wholly sinister figure which occupies the canvas, but which seems, with the completion of the study, to have disappeared entirely from the mind of its creator. It is equally remarkable that an inexperienced girl should have had independence and boldness enough to draw at full length a woman of the type of Lady Susan, and that, after she had

done so, the purity of her imagination and the delicacy of her taste should have prevented her from ever repeating the experiment.' [6]

'Purity of her imagination and the delicacy of her taste…'! This is to fall into the trap of believing Jane to be a paragon of primness. I can well imagine Lady Susan as an experimental avatar into which Jane extrapolates herself and gives herself dominion over men. Was this Jane exploring her 'dark side'? Fantasising about how, if she had possessed the prerequisite allure, she might exercise her intelligence in such dark arts? Again, how, in truth, could it be otherwise? The act of character creation requires projection into avatar-puppets who will dance to the author's tune, just as a reciprocal projection from readers is required if they are to have the satisfaction of vicariously experiencing the dance. The only real question is whether Jane liked and admired Lady Susan despite the character's amorality. *Lady Susan* is no cautionary tale, no polemic against want of virtue in a woman of beauty; we must conclude that Jane *did* like Lady Susan.

REFERENCES

1. *S&S*, ch. 23.

2. *P&P*, ch. 41.

3. *NA*, ch. 27.

4. B. C. Southam, *Jane Austen's Literary Manuscripts*, Oxford University Press, Oxford, 1964.

5. M. A. Austen-Leigh, *Personal Aspects of Jane Austen*, John Murray, London, 1920, https://archive.org/stream/personalaspectso004072mbp/personalaspectso004072mbp_djvu.txt, (date accessed 12.10.2020).

6. W. Austen-Leigh & R. A. Austen-Leigh, *Jane Austen, Her Life and Letters, A Family Record*, Smith, Elder & Co., London, 1913, ch. 5.

11

CASSANDRA'S FIRE

So, Cassandra resolves to destroy many of Jane's letters. How would she have done this? 'Obviously', in the fire. But it might not be such a straightforward matter: if you take a single piece of paper and fold it, Regency style, into itself – there being no envelopes, you will find that at the thickest point there are twelve thicknesses of paper! (A quarto sheet folded in half to make four pages would then be folded repeatedly to form a tab and receiving pocket.) The result is something of the order of 3mm thick. If we have 333 such letters, we would have a stack a metre high! Now, we do not know how many letters Cassandra kept, but we can be confident that she must have received at least a couple hundred from Jane.

Of the 160 letters published in Deirdre Le Faye's collection, [1] I count 96 as being to Cassandra. This collection identifies, from the typical pattern and frequency of letters between the sisters, where letters appear to be missing. Typically, when separated from Cassandra, letters from Jane would be at three to four-day intervals. From examining the dates of letters either side of the identified gaps we can estimate the number that are missing. This total does not include any gaps before or after a given sequence (since we do not have the corresponding dates), and does not include any sequences that are entirely missing, so we can be confident that the total is a low estimate. This gives me an estimate of 110. For those gaps before or after a sequence, there must be at least one letter missing; I make that a further 19, giving a grand total of at least 129 missing letters. (225 letters altogether.)

Given that the recipient paid the postage, and that this and the paper itself was not a trivial expense, we can assume that none of Jane's letters to Cassandra were short notes (and therefore candidates for immediate disposal); she would wait until successive entries gave sufficient length to warrant the postage.

There is also the question of Cassandra's letters to Jane: we can imagine Jane treasuring these and given reciprocity in their correspondence, we can be confident of a similar total number. As a legal matter these would all devolve to Cassandra under the terms of Jane's will. Possibly these were destroyed on Jane's death. But if Cassandra had any notion of there being a wider interest in Jane's letters to her, would she not see a wider interest in their reciprocals? I can only imagine that Cassandra was dismayed at the thought of her own correspondence being scrutinised and could not even bring herself to preserve them for release after her own death. (So, in combination with Jane's, a stack of well over a metre in height.)

Now disposal of these by burning is not a trivial matter unless you have a significant bonfire in the garden to toss them upon. In the novel *Miss Austen* by Gill Hornby, Cassandra plots to retrieve a stash of Jane's letters to Eliza Fowle (Cassandra's former fiancé's sister), and is looking forward to a bonfire: 'Oh, how she longed to be back in Chawton! She would have that bonfire, as soon as possible: feed the flames with those difficult letters; wait and watch until the ashes were cold.' [2] Now my instincts may be wildly askew here: perhaps the overwhelming concern was with the possible exposure; in which case a bonfire would certainly answer. I doubt that would be the approach however; too public, for even in a private garden the outdoor aspect would have the 'feel' of presenting an opportunity for public intrusion. And a garden bonfire would be too cavalier an approach; not admitting the solemnity of the event or lending due respect. I am more comfortable with the notion of a domestic fireplace with the letters being submitted to the flames reverentially – in the manner of a ritual sacrifice. These letters were keepsakes and of a kind that were truly 'of Jane'; they were literally from her hand and their significance was not merely from association in the manner of something she wore or otherwise possessed. Only a lock of hair might be thought comparably freighted. There is a reason that, before the digital age, a signature was the usual means of authentication. But with a large number of letters, disposal becomes quite an exercise. We might imagine Cassandra reading each one before its consignment to the flames; fine if there is half a dozen, not so fine if there is half a hundred and more. Easier if bundled and submitted as packages? But such bundles would take a significant time to burn; the ease with which an individual page will burn belies the difficulty of getting a sheaf to burn. (Ever tried burning a phone directory?) Many a secret has been retrieved from incompletely combusted documentation.

I cannot believe that the bundles would have been used as kindling; too utilitarian an approach and lacking in dignity. And it is inconceivable that the bundles would be provided to a servant to use in making up a fire; I believe instead that they must have been added to an established fire. And hundreds of letters would result in a great deal of ash and make for some housekeeping difficulty.

Now it is possible that Cassandra did not undertake this as a one-off event, it may have been the work of several days. And at age 70, presumably there was little else to occupy her? And she must still have had the wits and interest enough to undertake the task mindfully, since she did make a selection rather than simply disposing of them as a set, either to her nieces or to oblivion. Would the extended task have prolonged the agony? Would it be better, like removing a plaster, to suffer a swift sharp shock rather than endure the progressive teasing separation of individual committal? Given the practical difficulty, in the absence of a bonfire, I believe it must have been several days. And in such a matter it would be fitting to suffer some heartache; it would not be something to avoid but rather something to embrace. There would be the satisfaction of honouring her sister's memory with due reverence, and of a duty faithfully discharged.

A sitting room fire? A winter's evening (with less chance of disturbance)? A quiet time for reflection, and for mourning the loss of what was and what might have been?

We are told by Mr Austen-Leigh's sister Caroline, that of Jane's letters to Aunt Cassandra, '...My Aunt looked them over and burnt the greater part (as she told me), 2 or 3 years before her own death…' [3] Cassandra died at age 72. But her death seems to have been relatively sudden: she died at Godmersham after a stroke and was returned to Chawton for burial alongside her mother in St. Nicholas' Church. So, we have no reason to think that she was conscious of a marked decline in health 'two or three years before' that might have prompted her to act. She had kept the letters for nearly 30 years (Jane having died at age 41, when Cassandra was 43). Perhaps some remark or observation gave her cause to think of her own demise and the risk to Jane's memory of an uncensored release. Possibly it was Psalm 90; 'The days of our years are threescore years and ten…' Cassandra would be aware that, (certainly for the time) she was of a good age and the biblical milestone may have been just the catalyst she needed to bolster her resolve..

REFERENCES

1. D. Le Faye, *Jane Austen's Letters* (4th edition), Oxford University Press, Oxford, 2014.

2. G. Hornby, *Miss Austen*, Century, London, 2020, p.385.

3. J. E. Austen-Leigh, *A Memoir of Jane Austen and Other Family Recollections*, ed. Sutherland, Oxford University Press, Oxford, 2002, p. 174.

12

CASSANDRA'S SELECTION

In censoring Jane's letters, what would Cassandra's criteria have been? We are left with a legacy (beyond the books themselves) that is frustratingly thin. My immediate reaction is to rail at Cassandra's shade for denying us the motherlode. But I then remind myself that she was, by her own lights, honouring the memory of her beloved sister, and find myself ashamed of the impertinence of my perfect hindsight. And I reflect that Jane herself would have resented any intrusion into her personal life and would have considered it inappropriate.

As she has Anne Elliot observe in *Persuasion* regarding a letter shown to her:

> 'She was obliged to recollect that her seeing the letter was a violation of the laws of honour, that no one ought to be judged or to be known by such testimonies, that no private correspondence could bear the eye of others…' [1]

Yes, she would wish to be known as an accomplished authoress, but she would not have welcomed enquiries into her private life. Royalties yes; celebrity no! Not that I imagine she coveted material wealth; rather the financial security that would allow her to indulge a materially modest life of the mind. I imagine her at her happiest when at her writing desk and inhabiting, if only virtually, the likes of Highbury or Meryton. It seems that she wrote first to please herself; the subsequent acknowledgement that she possessed talent would lead to hope of wider regard (and larger income), but not the vacuous adoration of the masses.

So, on what basis would Cassandra select the letters to preserve? What would her feelings and priorities have been? It seems she was not concerned to preserve material for prosperity; that is surprising to our modern perspective but when Cassandra made her selection in the 1840s she would likely have no notion of posterity's interest in the letters; they would seem too peripheral, too trite, too removed from the magnum opus. After all, these were letters, not essays; they were composed as a succession of addenda from various times and days and not subject to revision and reworking. They have something of a stream of consciousness aspect to them:

> 'Benjamin Portal is here. How charming that is! – I do not exactly know why, but the phrase followed so naturally that I could not help putting it down.' [2]

It was only in 1870 that the first biography of Jane was published and the previously peripheral began to move towards centre stage.

Cassandra's concern would have been for those with a natural familial interest; the family and friends that knew Jane or were directly related to her and their collective memory of her. (Cassandra could not have foreseen a future in which her sister would be as routinely mentioned in similar terms of national heritage as Shakespeare and so celebrated as to appear on a bank note - an honour also shared by Shakespeare.) We may imagine she wanted to avoid anything that might cause pain or embarrassment to the family or that would not reflect well on Jane herself; anything that might be seen as mean-spirited. I suspect many (most? all?) of us, in a private exchange, will indulge in hyperbole for entertainment's sake – for dramatic effect. An outrageous remark, that would be completely unacceptable in polite, public society, may be commandeered to convey a truth; the understanding between the parties concerned allowing the package to be distinguished from its courier:

> 'Mrs Hall of Sherbourn was brought to bed yesterday of a dead child, some weeks before she expected, owing to a fright. – I suppose she happened unawares to look at her husband.' [3]

Funny because it is outrageous, but outside of the mutual understanding between the correspondents this would appear unfeeling and cruel. It is only because of our vicarious sharing of that understanding that we too can enjoy this remark without reservations.

In the introduction to her collection of Jane's letters, Deirdre Le Faye speculates:

'Close consideration shows that the destruction was probably because Jane either had described physical symptoms rather too fully (for example, during the autumn of 1798, when Cassandra was at Godmersham and Mrs Austen was ill at home in Steventon being nursed by Jane), or else because she had made some comment about other members of the family which Cassandra did not wish posterity to read.' [4]

But by no means was all the potentially hurtful or incendiary material expunged:

'If Miss Pearson should return with me, pray be careful not to expect too much beauty.' [5]

'Farmer Clarinbould died this morning, & I fancy Edward means to get some of his Farm if he can cheat Sir Brook enough in the agreement.' [6]

And consider this catalogue!

> 'There were very few Beauties, & such as there were, were not very handsome. Miss Iremonger did not look well, Mrs Blount was the only one much admired. She appeared exactly as she did in September, with the same broad face, diamond bandeau, white shoes, pink husband. & fat neck.— The two Miss Coxes were there; I traced in one the remains of the vulgar, broad featured girl who danced at Enham eight years ago;—the other is refined into a nice, composed looking girl like Catherine Bigg—I looked at Sir Champneys & thought of poor Rosalie; I looked at his daughter & thought her a queer animal with a white neck.—Mrs Warren, I was constrained to think a very fine young woman, which I much regret. She has got rid of some part of her child, & danced away with great activity, looking by no means very large.—Her

husband is ugly enough; uglier even than his cousin John; but he does not look so very old. The Miss Maitlands are both prettyish; very like Anne; with brown skins, large dark eyes, & a good deal of nose.—The General has got the Gout, & Mrs Maitland the Jaundice.—Miss Debary, Susan & Sally all in black, but without any Statues, made their appearance, & I was as civil to them as their bad breath would allow me.' [7]

Now it may be that when Cassandra destroyed the letters, perhaps as much as 30 years after they were written, she may have been satisfied that the remaining barbs would not injure anyone with any connection to the relations or friends to whom she gave or bequeathed the remainder. But by that point, with Jane an established literary figure, could she be confident that the remaining letters would not be used in evidence against Jane? On reading the letters and finding much, that outside that private channel, could still be seen as waspish, if not downright shrewish, I suspect that there was more to the selection than simply the avoidance of hurt feelings or the elimination of anything that could be construed as giving the lie to Jane's 'sweetness of temper' (the testimony of the epitaph from her brother James).

What is consistently absent? It strikes me that the remaining letters are all upbeat in tone: I find nothing that speaks of depression, nothing of chronically subdued spirits or anxiety. Yes, there are mentions of melancholic episodes, but they are just that – episodic. There is nothing that contradicts the inference that might be drawn from the books that the authoress was of a good-humoured nature. And yet for two sisters that were so very close (Cassandra: '...I had not a thought concealed from her...' [8]), it seems unlikely that there would not sometimes be a downbeat tone? Was this then the basis for rejection? There is no introspection, no self-examination or reflection. Was this universally absent or selected for rejection?

It has many times been remarked that there is an absence of politics, but I don't believe anyone imagines politics a criterion for rejection; I judge it more likely that the absence of politics was universal, it being an area unsuitable for an exchange of letters between two intimates that would have opportunity to discuss such abstract concerns face-to-face when a directly interactive conversation would be more effective. Given that they were usually together, I can see that the letters would tend towards reporting rather than debating, and that interactive written exchanges would focus on the concrete (which ribbon to buy) rather than the abstract (which policy to buy into).

REFERENCES

1. *Persuasion*, ch. 21.
2. Letter No. 21, 11 June 1799.
3. Letter No. 10, 27 October 1798.
4. D. Le Faye, *Jane Austen's Letters* (4th edition), Oxford University Press, Oxford, 2014, p.xiii.
5. Letter No. 7, 18 September 1796.
6. Letter No. 5, 5 September 1796.
7. Letter No. 27, 20 November 1800
8. Letter CEA/1, 29 July 1817.

13

JANE'S DOOR

There is a well-loved and often repeated story that in Chawton Cottage there was a creaking swing-door that Jane refused to have fixed because it alerted her to an approach. The source is her nephew's memoir:

> 'She was careful that her occupation should not be suspected by servants, or visitors, or any persons beyond her own family party. She wrote upon small sheets of paper which could easily be put away, or covered with a piece of blotting paper. There was, between the front door and the offices, a swing door which creaked when it was opened; but she objected to having this little inconvenience remedied, because it gave her notice when anyone was coming...I have no doubt that I and my sisters and cousins, in our visits to Chawton, frequently disturbed this mystic process, without having any idea of the mischief that we were doing; certainly we never should have guessed it by any signs of impatience or irritability in the writer.' [1]

A charming story, but are we to make of it? From creak to appearance we may estimate two, perhaps three seconds? What might be done in this time? It would not be possible to hide all evidence of writing; where would you hide quill-pen, ink well, paper? These accoutrements would mean there was no possibility of unceremoniously sweeping all into a drawer.

Yes, she might cover the work in hand with blotting paper or other material, but this would likely only excite the curiosity of the intruder. Even if Jane were able to successfully hide her work, that is not to say she could hide her activity. The attempt would likely leave her flustered; it is difficult to remain perfectly composed when acting hurriedly under pressure to hide a secret. And why should she make the attempt? Far more practical to use camouflage by having a partly composed letter to hand. And I do not imagine visitors would arrive unannounced - she would be unlikely to be surprised by her nephews and nieces or any other non-resident.

For the most part, the 'intruders' would be sister/mother/Martha Lloyd[a] who were in on the secret anyway. The servants would just see their mistress at her writing table and think nothing of it. Consider the number of 'false alarms' there would be. And anyway, there was no secret about Jane being a writer, the 'secret' was that she was a published authoress. To see Jane or 'the mistress' writing would be completely unremarkable; more remarkable to see her *not* writing if she were at leisure. I think we can safely dismiss the story as fable.

I can imagine someone saying, 'We must get that door fixed' and in a throwaway remark Jane replying, 'We must do no

---

[a] Jane's life-long friend who lived with the family at Chawton Cottage.

such thing – it lets me know when someone is coming!' This then becoming conflated with her reticence to establish a piece of family folklore.

REFERENCES

1. J. E. Austen-Leigh, *A Memoir of Jane Austen and Other Family Recollections*, ed. Sutherland, Oxford University Press, Oxford, 2002, p. 81.

JANE'S VOICE

We cannot know what Jane sounded like, but in a very real sense it is still possible for us to 'hear' her. Not the timbre of her voice, it is true, but her manner of speaking. In demonstration of this, consider the following passage:

> 'While I'll try to put Jane back into her social class and time, I must admit that I also write as a signed up 'Janeite', a devotee and worshipper. I too have searched for my own Jane, and naturally I have found her to be simply a far, far better version of myself: clever, kind, funny, but also angry at the restrictions of her life, someone tirelessly searching for ways to be free and creative. I know who I *want* Jane Austen to be, and I put my cards on the table. This is, unashamedly, the story of my Jane. Every word of it written with love.'

Do you recognise this voice? It is one familiar to many from her programmes on television and radio. It is Lucy Worsley's. The passage is drawn from the introduction to her book, *Jane Austen at Home.* [1] In reading her books (as with others written by familiar figures from television and radio), I find the speech patterns, the use of idioms and metaphors, the emphasis, the 'tone' all contribute to a distinctive style that one can 'hear' in her written text.

When Jane was writing to her sister Cassandra, her approach was conversational. The letters are, most definitely, not studied, structured essays. They are spontaneous and entirely informal. Jane herself once wrote to Cassandra, 'I have now attained the true art of letter-writing, which we are always told, is to express on paper exactly what one would say to the same person by word of mouth.' [2]

Others of Jane's letters are more formal and business-like, or less confiding, but those to Cassandra are open and uninhibited.

Here is an example. I have retained the dashes and under linings which give some idea of emphasis but have expanded the contractions and adjusted[a] the spelling and punctuation that would otherwise make her 'harder to hear'. The significance of many of the references she makes is lost to us, but that is of no matter for my purpose. She writes (at age 37) from home at Chawton Cottage to Cassandra who is staying in Steventon:

'Sunday Evening, 24th January 1813

My dear Cassandra,

This is exactly the weather we could wish for, if you are but well enough to enjoy it. I shall be glad to hear that you are not confined to the house by an increase of cold. Mr Digweed has used us basely. Handsome

---

[a] I am not so impertinent as to say 'corrected'. In two-hundred years, orthodoxies can change.

is as handsome does; he is therefore a very ill-looking man. I hope you have sent off a letter to me by this day's post, unless you are tempted to wait till tomorrow by one of Mr Chute's franks.—We have had no letter since you went away, and no visitor, except Miss Benn who dined with us on Friday; but we have received the half of an excellent Stilton cheese—we presume, from Henry.—My mother is very well and finds great amusement in the glove-knitting; when this pair is finished, she means to knit another, and at present wants no other work. – We quite run over with books. <u>She</u> has got Sir John Carr's *Travels in Spain* from Miss B. and I am reading a Society-Octavo,[b] an *Essay on the Military Police & Institutions of the British Empire*, by Capt. Pasley of the Engineers, a book which I protested against at first, but which upon trial I find delightfully written and highly entertaining. I am as much in love with the author as I ever was with Clarkson or Buchanan, or even the two Mr Smiths of the city. The first soldier I ever sighed for; but he does write with extraordinary force and spirit. Yesterday moreover brought us Mrs Grant's letters, with Mr White's compliments.—But I have disposed of them, compliments and all, for the first fortnight to Miss Papillon and among so many readers or retainers of books as we have in Chawton, I dare say there will be no difficulty in getting rid of them for another fortnight if necessary.—I learn from Sir J. Carr that there is no Government House at Gibraltar.—l must

[b] A book from the Alton Book Society

alter it to the Commissioner's.[c]—Our party on Wednesday was not unagreeable, though as usual we wanted a better Master of the House, one less anxious and fidgetty, and more conversable. In consequence of a civil note that morning from Mrs Clement, I went with her and her husband in their tax-cart; —civility on both sides; I would rather have walked, and no doubt, <u>they</u> must have wished I had.—I ran home with my own dear Thomas[d] at night in great luxury. Thomas was very useful. We were eleven altogether, as you will find on computation, adding Miss Benn and two strange gentlemen, a Mr Twyford, curate of Great Worldham who is living in Alton, and his friend Mr Wilkes.—I do not know that Mr T. is anything, except very dark-complexioned, but Mr W. was a useful addition, being an easy, talking, pleasantish young man;—a <u>very</u> young man, hardly 20 perhaps. He is of St Johns, Cambridge, and spoke very highly of H. Walter as a scholar; —he said he was considered as the best classic in the University.—How such a report would have interested my father!—I could see nothing very promising between Mr P. and Miss P.T.—She placed herself on one side of him at first, but Miss Benn obliged her to move up higher;—and she had an empty plate, and even asked him to give her some mutton without being attended to for some time.—There might be design in this, to be sure, on his side;—he

---

[c] In *MP*

[d] Chawton Cottage manservant

might think an empty stomach the most favourable for love.—Upon Mrs Digweed's mentioning that she had sent the *Rejected Addresses*[e] to Mr Hinton, I began talking to her a little about them and expressed my hope of their having amused her. Her answer was, "Oh! dear, yes, very droll indeed;—the opening of the house!—and the striking up of the fiddles!"—What she meant, poor woman, who shall say?—I sought no farther.—The Papillons have now got the book and like it very much; their niece Eleanor has recommended it most warmly to them.—<u>She</u> looks like a 'rejected addresser'. As soon as a whist party was formed and a round table threatened, I made my mother an excuse, and came away; leaving just as many for <u>their</u> round table, as there were at Mrs Grants.[f]—I wish they might be as agreeable a set.—It was past 10 when I got home, so I was not ashamed of my dutiful delicacy.—The Coulthards were talked of you may be sure; no end of <u>them</u>; Miss Terry had heard they were going to rent Mr Bramston's house at Oakley, and Mrs Clement that they were going to live at Streatham.— Mrs Digweed and I agreed that the house at Oakley could not possibly be large enough for them, and now we find they have really taken it.—Mr Gauntlett is thought very agreeable, and there are <u>no</u> children at all.—The Miss Sibleys want to establish a book society in their side of the country, like ours. What

---

[e] A collection of parodies of contemporary poets by the 'two Mr Smiths of the city'.
[f] In *MP*

can be a stronger proof of that superiority in ours over the Steventon & Manydown Society, which I have always foreseen and felt?—No emulation of the kind was ever inspired by <u>their</u> proceedings; no such wish of the Miss Sibleys was ever heard, in the course of the many years of that society's existence;—And what are their Biglands and their Barrows, their Macartneys & Mackenzies, to Capt. Pasley's *Essay on the Military Police of the British Empire*, and the rejected addresses? I have walked once to Alton, and yesterday Miss Papillon and I walked together to call on the Garnets. She invited herself very pleasantly to be my companion, when I went to propose to her the indulgence of accommodating us about the letters from the mountains. <u>I</u> had a very agreeable walk; if <u>she</u> had not more shame for her, for I was quite as entertaining as she was. Dame G. is pretty well, and we found her surrounded by her well-behaved, healthy, large-eyed children.—I took her an old shift and promised her a set of our linen; and my companion left some of her bank stock with her. Tuesday has done its duty, and I have had the pleasure of reading a very comfortable letter. It contains so much, that I feel obliged to write down the whole of this page and perhaps something in a cover.—When my parcel is finished I shall walk with it to Alton. I believe Miss Benn will go with me. She spent yesterday evening with us.—As I know Mary is interested in her not being neglected by her neighbours, pray tell her that Miss B. dined last Wednesday at Mr Papillons—on Thursday with

Capt. and Mrs Clement—Friday here—Saturday with Mrs Digweed—and Sunday with the Papillons again.—I had fancied that Martha would be at Barton from last Saturday, but am best pleased to be mistaken. I hope she is now quite well.—Tell her that I hunt away the rogues every night from under her bed; they feel the difference of her being gone.— Miss Benn wore her new shawl last night, sat in it the whole evening and seemed to enjoy it very much. — "A very sloppy lane" last Friday!—What an odd sort of country you must be in!ᵍ I cannot at all understand it! It was just greasy here on Friday, in consequence of the little snow that had fallen in the night.—Perhaps it <u>was</u> cold on Wednesday, yes, I believe it certainly was—but nothing terrible.— Upon the whole, the weather for winter-weather is delightful, the walking excellent.—I cannot imagine what sort of a place Steventon can be!—My Mother sends her love to Mary, with thanks for her kind intentions and enquiries as to the pork, and will prefer receiving her share from the two <u>last</u> pigs.— She has great pleasure in sending her a pair of garters, and is very glad that she had them ready knit.—Her Letter to Anna is to be forwarded, if any opportunity offers; otherwise it may wait for her return.—Mrs Leigh's letter came this morning—We are glad to hear anything so tolerable of Scarlets.— Poor Charles and his frigate. But there could be no

---

ᵍ The point being that Steventon is only twelve miles from Chawton. Presumably, "A very sloppy lane" is a quotation from Cassandra's previous letter to Jane.

chance of his having one, while it was thought such a certainty.—l can hardly believe Brother Michael's news; we have no such idea in Chawton at least.— Mrs Bramstone is the sort of woman I detest.—Mr Cottrell is worth ten of her. It is better to be given the lie direct, than to excite no interest...[*last leaf of letter missing.*]' [3]

In this we hear her wry, ironical, good-humoured voice. A good-natured soul ready to greet the world and human folly with a smile rather than a frown.

'Let other pens dwell on guilt and misery. I quit such odious subjects as soon as I can, impatient to restore everybody not greatly in fault themselves to tolerable comfort, and to have done with all the rest.' [4]

REFERENCES

1. L. Worsley, *Jane Austen at Home*, Hodder & Stoughton, London, 2017.
2. Letter No. 29, 5 January 1801.
3. Letter No. 78, 24 January 1813.
4. *MP*, Ch. 48.

15

JANE'S CHAMBER POT

There is an intricate delicacy to Jane's work, that 'fine brush (on ivory)' that is at the heart of her appeal for her readers; the refined sensibilities that are exhibited by her protagonists, the nice distinctions of manner by which her characters engage with one another. It can be difficult to square this with the indelicacies of regency life; the sheer, practical rudeness (in the sense of 'lacking refinement') of daily existence when compared with our modern expectations; the absence of running water, the rudimentary sanitation, the omnipresent horse dung (and worse), the sights and smells of animal husbandry, the difficulties of bodily and oral hygiene, the absence of female hygiene products. No washing machines, no automatic dish washers, no refrigeration, no damp proof courses for buildings or people (no anti-perspirants). Jane once wrote, 'What dreadful hot weather we have! It keeps me in a continual state of inelegance.' [1] She writes elegantly of inelegance!

Jo Baker's novel '*Longbourn*' is an interesting corrective in providing a reworking of *P&P* from the perspective of the servants wherein these everyday realities form part of the warp and weft of the story:

'Sarah carried a chamber pot down from the

82

Bennets' room, crossing the landing towards the narrow back stairs. She went carefully, head turned aside. Just nightwater, thankfully; not the dreadful slopping thunk of solids.' [2]

I question that 'dreadful'? I suspect there would have been no 'dread', just an everyday acceptance of unpleasantness – the likely subject of coarse humour between the servants. Of the laundry:

"And there are the napkins to do, too' Sarah added. It had been that unfortunate time of the month, when all the women of the house had been more than usually short-tempered, clumsy and prone to tears, and then had bled. The napkins now soaked in a separate tub that smelt uneasily of the butcher's shop; they'd be boiled last, in the dregs of the copper, before it was emptied.' [3]

Given the practical difficulties, it seems likely women of the gentry would undertake a self-imposed purdah during that 'unfortunate time of the month'; no dinner parties, no attendance at assemblies, no promenading. The continued activity promise of modern sanitary products would have been unthinkable. Presumably these episodes of indisposition would simply be explained away as 'feeling unwell'.

But how do we reconcile the use of a chamber pot or the outside 'necessary house' with the refinement of manners in the drawing room? There is, with our modern sensibilities, an immediate recoiling from the conjunction. But be the sensibilities modern or Georgian, the plumbing sophisticated or absent, I suspect that the imperative of bodily functions has remained a potential social embarrassment; our regency forbears would also have recoiled. There is an evolutionary instinct that prompts us, in answering the call of nature, to seek privacy to avoid physical vulnerability and the hazards of pathogens and this instinct becomes codified in manners that are accepted by the tribe (society). The regency population were inevitably obliged to confront these concerns more directly than we, but would nevertheless I believe, have had the same understanding about the exclusion of such matters from polite conversation. There must have been a corresponding understanding between servants and served about the degree of notice (if any) between them of bodily functions.

Other than avoidance, the other 'coping mechanism' is to make these joking matters. There is a spectrum here; from the deliberately coarse, through the merely vulgar, to affected and 'polite' euphemism, on to oblique reference and unspoken understanding.

This is viewed by some, particularly those that routinely employ the left hand of my spectrum, as having a reciprocal spectrum of hypocritical snobbishness. But this is simplistic; being able to delegate and distance oneself from unpleasantness does not make one a snob - it is the assumption that it is innate worth rather than circumstance that allows the distance.

There is an apparent discrepancy between the polite constraints in Jane's novels and the licence more generally accepted in cartoons, plays and novels of the time. The bawdiness and explicit references in Gillray's cartoons, Elizabeth Inchbald's play *The Lovers' Vows*[a] and Fielding's novel *The Adventures of Tom Jones* refute any idea that prudishness and primness (and hypocrisy) were characteristic of the era; the Georgians (logically enough) were not Victorian in their sensibilities. Jane herself enjoyed works that were distinctly risqué but evidently had no notion of incorporating any such aspect in her own. Yet there are references to licentiousness; consider the 'off stage/page' behaviour of Wickham and Willoughby, Lydia Bennet and Mary Crawford. And there is Mary Crawford's infamous joke in *MP*: 'Certainly, my home at my uncle's brought me acquainted with a circle of admirals. Of Rears and Vices I saw enough. Now do not be suspecting me of a pun, I entreat.' [4] There is continuing debate about whether this is a reference to homosexual practice or the 'English vice' of spanking but either way, the oblique sexual reference stands.

I love the playful challenge in this; the fact of the pun is undeniable, we are entreated not to suspect Mary of having deliberately made it, which naturally we immediately do. I have a notion that this is Jane the ventriloquist at work; it is really her sardonic voice we hear.

Jane was no prude, she did not shun the ribald, and we cannot imagine it beyond her skill, but she chose not to embrace it for her own art, presumably because she found it would not serve her purpose.

---

[a] As referenced in *MP*.

REFERENCES

1. Letter No. 7, 18 September 1796.
2. J. Baker, *Longbourn*, Black Swan, London, 2014, p.33.
3. *Ibid.* p.17.
4. *MP*, ch. 6.

16

TWO LETTERS

I have mentioned in Chapter 12 that many of Jane's letters have something of the quality of a stream of consciousness about them; they are not composed as structured essays around a distinct theme or subject. This is only to be expected in personal correspondence between family and friends of course, but this style separates these letters from her familiar published works. It seems unlikely that they would have been drafted first and then a final fair copy made for posting, and in that respect, they are remarkable for the fluency that they nevertheless exhibit. Perhaps of particular interest in this regard are the two letters Jane wrote to her brother Francis (Frank) announcing the death of their father. These letters were written on consecutive days and have essentially the same content, relating the course of the fatal illness, the point being that they were directed differently: the first to Dungeness, the second to Portsmouth, since Francis was commanding officer of HMS *Leopard*.

Consider the delicacy with which the sad news is imparted in each (I preserve the textual idiosyncrasies):

'Monday 21 January 1805

My dearest Frank,

I have melancholy news to relate, & sincerely feel for your feelings under the shock of it. – I wish I could better prepare You for it. – But having said so much, Your mind will already forestall the sort of Event which I have to communicate. Our dear Father has closed his virtuous & happy life, in a death almost as free from suffering as his Children could have wished… [1]

'Tuesday 22 January 1805

My dearest Frank,

I wrote to you yesterday; but your letter to Cassandra this morning, by which we learn the probability of your being by this time at Portsmouth, obliges me to write to you again, having unfortunately a communication as necessary as painful to make to you. – Your affectionate heart will be greatly wounded, & I wish the shock could have been lessen'd by a better preparation; – but the Event has been sudden, & so must be the information of it. We have lost an Excellent Father…' [2]

It is perhaps surprising that Jane does not repeat the phrases of the first letter; having composed them on Monday, it would seem natural for them to still echo in her mind on Tuesday, but she finds new phrasing conveying the same sentiment. They both appear 'crafted', but it seems unlikely there would have been the time or emotional energy available to dedicate to the task. Which, if truly the case, demonstrates an extraordinary fluency to her eloquence; it seems she had such a ready command of language that she could, in short order, conjure apposite phrasing. And this at a time when she must have been feeling keen distress in her grief; the first was written on the same day that her father died and presumably after little or no sleep. The imperative was to relay the news to her brothers. And it is interesting that the task fell to Jane. She says in the first letter, 'And tomorrow we shall I dare say have the comfort of James's presence, as an Express has been sent to him. – We write also of course to Godmersham & Brompton', so to brothers Edward and Henry, respectively. Possibly, there was a division of labour in the household: did Cassandra and her mother also write, or was correspondence delegated to Jane, as the one best equipped to handle it, whilst they concerned themselves with other matters?

REFERENCES

1. Letter No. 40, 21 January 1805.
2. Letter No. 41, 22 January 1805.

JANE'S LABORATORY

The implicit criticism of 'domestic theatricals' in *MP* is so sustained and closely argued that it is difficult to believe Jane did not herself hold those views. And yet we know she took an active part in the amateur dramatic events at Steventon, and as late as 1808 she was playing Mrs Candour in Sheridan's *School for Scandal* with the Bigg-Wither family at Manydown. How are we to explain the apparent discrepancy?

The staging of *Lover's Vows* in the billiard room at Mansfield Park is a marvellous vehicle for developing the drama of the book itself; it is this drama-within-a-drama that allows an accelerated development of character interaction. It is in their attempts to resolve the tensions, both personal and inter-person, arising from the staging of the play that the characters effectively declare their individual manifestos. Whatever Jane's personal views, if this vehicle were to serve its novelistic purpose, these tensions could not be denied and, of course, it is possible to enjoy all sorts of things without necessarily approving of them.

Given her active involvement it surely must be that Jane was not critical of private theatricals *per se*, but rather of the casting of individuals to parts that gave them inappropriate licence, or of the self-interested behaviour that could be invoked. 'Surely', in that I must believe Jane incapable of what would otherwise be blatant hypocrisy. All may be well if the staging of the play remains the focus,[a] but if this is not the case and the players bring or develop their own romantic agendas, then there are distinct hazards. Players will have licence to literally rehearse a degree of intimacy that would only normally be approached progressively through mutual regard and validation of reciprocated feelings. As demonstration of this, we need only consider Mary Crawford's provocative, 'What gentlemen among you am I to have the pleasure of making love to?' [1] when the question of casting for the part of Anhalt arises.

To modern sensibilities these concerns may seem misplaced or exaggerated, but in Jane's time impropriety was less readily excused and respectability more prized and difficult to recover.

In addition to the hazards of accelerated intimacy there are those of competing egos fighting for recognition, acclaim, and ascendancy. In truth there is no difference in this regard with wider social interactions outside the world of amateur dramatics; it is only that the spatial and temporal compression of the stage foments an intensity that is normally absent.

In her book *Jane & Dorothy*, Marian Veevers makes the point that Jane gives, 'an unflinching insider's view of everything

---

[a] I was tempted to write 'as long as the play's the thing', but that would be a distortion of Shakespeare's purpose in *Hamlet* – in that drama-within-a-drama, the play is 'the thing' to expose Hamlet's mother's guilt.

that is worst about amateur acting' and that,

> 'There can be no doubt that this detailed understanding of what can happen among a group of people – even people who are fond of one another – when 'the inclination to act is awakened' [2] came from real observation.' [3]

Veevers concludes:

> 'Jane's distrust of amateur theatricals, rather than being founded on prudery, seems to have arisen from a much more humane concern that the opportunity to perform released a tide of self-obsession which could temporarily render even kindly people insensitive to the feelings and needs of others.' [4]

It is notable that in *MP* Jane does not attempt to qualify the implicit criticism in terms of circumstance; the individuals involved, the nature of the play, the societal context, although these all bear on the realisation of the hazards. She does not distinguish the Mansfield Park production from the generality of amateur productions, presumably because she considered it typical and a fair representation of the difficult waters to be navigated.

Jane does not so much argue against the 'playroom' as the 'hothouse'. The home theatre was a laboratory in which the seed crystal of character would grow in a supersaturated solution and make its nature and flaws apparent.

REFERENCES

1. *MP*, ch. 15.
2. *MP*, ch. 13.
3. M. Veevers, *Jane and Dorothy: A True Tale of Sense and Sensibility*, Sandstone Press Ltd, Ross-shire, 2017, p. 49.
4. *Ibid.*, p. 50.

18

JANE'S ORPHANS

Why abandon *The Watsons*?[a] There is the curious extended period centred on her years in Bath and Southampton where Jane does not appear to substantially progress with her writing. There has been speculation that she was too unhappy or too busy to write. I do not subscribe to such notions. Jane was made to write; it was a core part of her being. And not just the transmutation of evanescent thought to enduring words on the page; I suspect she found the physical act of penmanship comforting. There may be an absence of evidence, but once again I am not persuaded in this matter that this constitutes significant evidence of absence. I do not imagine her confined to correspondence and it seems she was continually honing her material: she was still editing her juvenilia at age 35. *Lady Susan* (as distinct from the *Susan* that was to become *NA*) was completed as a fair copy in 1805 but started in 1793 at age seventeen. And I imagine it could be a slow business; to craft an aphorism to hit exactly the right tone would not be the work of a few minutes.

A variety of reasons have been postulated but none seems

---

[a] Work on the novel was begun by Jane in 1803 and only five chapters were completed.

compelling and there is no conclusive evidence:

Claire Tomalin speculates that Jane was depressed during her time in Bath, and finds suggestions to support this in her letters, and couples this with a plausible reaction to the dislocation from her home and established domestic routine. [1]

Lucy Worsley, although finding Tomalin's work of 'great perception and subtlety' wonders whether this is to misplace transference of the emotional response of a twenty-first century woman, and offers instead the idea that the story was abandoned because it touched on too many regrets from Jane's life. [2]

Were the circumstances related in *The Watsons* too close for comfort, particularly given the sudden death of her father? I do not find the circumstances are especially close to Jane's. At the end of the fragment the manuscript relates the circumstances of Emma, the protagonist:

> 'The change in her home, society, and style of life, in consequence of the death of one friend and the imprudence of another, had indeed been striking. From being the first object of hope and solicitude to an uncle who had formed her mind with the care of a parent, and of tenderness to an aunt whose amiable temper had delighted to give her every indulgence; from being the life and spirit of a house where all had been comfort and elegance, and the expected heiress of an easy independence, she was become of importance to no one,—a burden on those whose affections she could not expect, an addition in a

house already overstocked, surrounded by inferior minds, with little chance of domestic comfort, and as little hope of future support. It was well for her that she was naturally cheerful, for the change had been such as might have plunged weak spirits in despondence.' [3]

It is true that the note in J. E. Leigh's memoir reports of the plot development outline, that Emma's father 'was soon to die', [4] but that aside, the parallels with Jane's circumstances appear superficial. I am reminded of the reader of a newspaper horoscope column, actively looking for opportunities to invoke confirmation bias.

It may be that the successive blows of the death of her friend and mentor, Mrs Lefroy, in a horse riding accident on 16th December 1804, and the sudden death of her father on 21st January 1805 did have a bearing on her abandonment of *The Watsons*. However, Claire Harman in her book *Jane's Fame*, makes the point that despite the family trauma of the death of Cassandra's fiancé in 1797, Jane managed to complete *First Impressions*.[b] [5]

It has also been suggested that she was simply too busy with the social whirl of Bath or that domestic arrangements and demands were not conducive to her writing.

Perhaps the work did not please, and other projects held more appeal? Despite being not as polished as her completed works, *The Watsons* looks like a solid start and the outline reported for the development of the plot seems to hold

---

[b] The precursor to *P&P*.

promise. This appears to us to be a substantial investment of time and effort. But perhaps it did not to Jane. When we look at the speed with which she worked in later years at Chawton, is it possible that Jane did not see it that way? Perhaps the investment had not reached 'the point of no return'? Possibly we should not see the work as 'abandoned' but rather as 'dormant': the manuscript was preserved, and it may be that Jane anticipated she would return to the work at some point. Although a possibly telling point against this is her adoption of the name 'Emma' for another of her heroines. Yes, she might change the name readily enough (as she did with Susan/Catherine for *NA* because of another publication's use of the name Susan) but if not obliged by the competition, why give yourself the trouble?

We should remember that at this point Jane was not yet a published author; it may be that given the false starts with *First Impressions* and *Susan/NA* she was not persuaded that she ever would be? (Reason enough to be depressed we might think.) She had no publisher or established readership to please, no deadline to meet. She was writing primarily to please herself.

And, of course, there does not have to be a single compelling reason; it may have been a combination of factors, such as those identified, that prevailed in different combinations at different times. Perhaps we look too hard?

REFERENCES

1. C. Tomalin, *Jane Austen: A Life*, Penguin Books, London, 2000, p. 175.

2. L. Worsley, *Jane Austen at Home*, Hodder & Stoughton, London, 2017, p. 198.

3. *The Watsons*, ch. 6.

4. J. E. Austen-Leigh, *A Memoir of Jane Austen,* Macmillan and Co., Ltd., London, 1906, p.364

5. C. Harman, *Jane's Fame*, Canongate Books, Edinburgh, 2009, p. 36.

19

JANE'S FACE

What did Jane look like? What would we give for a photograph? (Or better still a video!) Does the image on the £10 note first issued in 2017 get anywhere near the truth?

The evidence is thin: a sketch by Cassandra, some limited recollections from family and friends. Nevertheless, let us see what we can make of this. The sketch by Cassandra is estimated by the National Portrait Gallery to be from circa 1810 when Jane would have been 35.

It is this sketch that was 'adapted' (I hesitate to say 'enhanced') as a watercolour portrait by James Andrews in 1869, which was itself subsequently the basis of an engraving (by the Scottish firm of Lizars), both under commission from Jane's nephew, James Edward Austen-Leigh, for his memoir of Jane. It is this engraving that is the basis of the image on the £10 banknote. Presumably, the image conformed with Victorian sensibilities and wish fulfilment, but to my 'new Elizabethan' sensibilities it has a 'saccharine' doll-like appearance that positively offends in not conveying anything of Jane's intelligence and acerbic wit. Not that such qualities can necessarily be determined from appearance but an impression of them may be so suggested.

The most direct evidence must be the original sketch, which is, frankly, a disappointment; it borders on the grotesque. It seems Cassandra had no particular skill as a portraitist, but that in itself may give us some clues. What mistakes, typically, would an amateur make? What would they be likely to get right, or nearly so? From other work that Cassandra left it does not appear that she was completely inept.

To suggest answers, I consulted my wife (an accomplished botanical artist) who has an endearing trait of scribbling impromptu portraits on our daily newspaper in something of a David Downton fashion model portrait style; the merest pen stroke suggesting a curve here and there, an intimation of shadow, the suggestion of depth, the arch of a brow.

It seems an approximation to the overall shape of the head might be expected, together with something of the hair line. These form relatively conspicuous outlines. The features and their placement are rather more subtle; an attempt to directly draw them in the two dimensions available will typically fail; the approach must be to 'suggest' them and allow the viewer's brain to infer the third dimension.

So, a roundish, oval head? The eyebrows we might assume to be reasonably accurate; so thin and not highly arched. The long nose appears consistent with the images we have of her siblings. The mouth, small and thin lipped, may not be accurately placed or proportioned but we might presume these characteristics faithful. Similarly, the eyes may not be properly placed or proportioned but we might presume the relatively round shape to be a true characteristic. The bags under the eyes are not heavy but presumably the attempt at reproduction was prompted by some such aspect.

The neck certainly appears too thick, the eyes too large; the ear too far back; classic errors of the amateur.

The sketch does appear consistent in the essentials with such recollections as we have (is it possible they were influenced by the sketch?):

From her nephew James-Edwards' memoir:

> 'In person she was very attractive; her figure was rather tall and slender, her step light and firm, and her whole appearance expressive of health and animation. In complexion she was a clear brunette with a rich colour; she had full round cheeks, with mouth and nose small and well formed, bright hazel eyes, and brown hair forming natural curls close around her face. If not so regularly handsome as her sister, yet her countenance had a peculiar charm of its own to the eyes of most beholders.' [1]

The reference to a 'small nose' seems questionable given the characteristic shown in other Austen family portraits.

Her brother Henry: 'Her features were separately good. Their assemblage produced an unrivalled expression of that cheerfulness, sensibility, and benevolence, which were her real characteristics.' [2] Rather faint and consequently damning praise?

It seems there is agreement that she was tall and slender.

These recollections may not have been entirely candid and

may have tended towards a flattering portrait if only to avoid being seen as ungenerous in speaking of a relative. It seems certain that Jane was not judged beautiful or 'handsome' or we would likely have some explicit record of this and perhaps a professional, commissioned portrait.

There is no mention of her hands, but it would seem likely that her fingernails and fingertips would have been routinely blackened by ink from the use of a quill pen?

Several artists have attempted representation, but I find most disappoint in one respect or another; they either bring attested attributes to implausible prominence or have an appearance that is generic and regular to the point of insipidity. To my mind, the most plausible piece is a bust by sculptress Suzie Zamit. This is subtly informed by the family portraits and descriptions and, unlike many representations, looks as if it could have been drawn from live sittings; hence my 'most plausible'. This has inspired the pencil sketch by my wife that is reproduced here.

*Pencil sketch of Jane by Linda Dearden, inspired by Suzie Zamit's
sculpture*

Given the disappointment of Cassandra's sketch, it is perhaps surprising that it was not discarded? Perhaps the sisters enjoyed laughing at the woeful attempt and a happy memory was formed that prompted its safe keeping? It seems unlikely that it would have been kept if was considered hurtful.

Of course, these are all *static* considerations; they offer nothing of the *dynamic*. We are all aware of people who are not considered conventionally beautiful but who nevertheless have a powerful attractiveness arising from a beguiling play of form and features. There is much fanciful talk of eyes 'sparkling' and the like, but such terms are a metaphorical attempt to capture the effect rather than the physical reality. The shift of the gaze, the arch of the brows, the turn of the mouth, the tilt of the head, the fall of the hair, a qualifying gesture with the hand; the coquette will deliberately employ these elements (and more!) to be flirtatious, but they may also be unconscious attributes of the persona that may take on additional potency when married with witty and intelligent conversation. We may imagine that in company, if her interest were engaged, Jane would have 'sparkled'.

If we are to believe Harris Bigg-Wither did propose, we might reasonably ask why? He was a young man (twenty-one) with an estate to inherit, and despite his stammer he would presumably be considered a 'good catch' with a correspondingly large number of prospective anglers. Why would he choose to make an offer to impoverished Jane? I like to think he saw 'sparkle' and was understandably beguiled.

Suzie Zamit's sculpture of Jane

(By kind permission of Suzie Zamit)

REFERENCES

1. J. E. Austen-Leigh, *A Memoir of Jane Austen and Other Family Recollections*, ed. Sutherland, Oxford University Press, Oxford, 2002, p. 70.
2. Biographical Notice of the Author by Henry Austen, 1818 in *Ibid.,* p. 139.

20

JANE'S GOD

The book *On the Origin of Species by Means of Natural Selection, or the Preservation of Favoured Races in the Struggle for Life*, (more popularly known, understandably, as *The Origin of Species*) by Charles Darwin, was published by Jane's publisher, John Murray, in 1859.

It was the first formal exposition of what is known as the 'theory of evolution'.[a] This first publication was many years after Jane's death, and she could have no notion of the revolutionary theory that countered the 'argument by design' for God's existence. This argument posits that the variety and complexity of life forms and their intricate interlocking within the natural world, makes it clear that there must be a 'designer' that had conceived and engineered the 'design'.

To Jane and her contemporaries, the wonder of the natural world would make it appear self-evident that there was a God. And she was immersed in the Anglican orthodoxy, and her faith would be continually reinforced by the beliefs and

---

[a] The term 'theory' has led some to insist that it is merely a conjectured hypothesis, but that is a misunderstanding of the scientific use of the term theory. I refer the interested reader to Richard Dawkins *et al.*

practices of those around her. I do not suggest Jane would have been incapable of independent thought in this, but she was perhaps unlikely to meet anything to prompt this, other than the apparent capriciousness with which death and misfortune might befall even those that seemed to lead blameless lives (and the theologians stood (and remain) ready to explain this). Her world was pervaded by Anglicanism; it was so integrated into her existence, so much part of the warp and weft of her life, that it would likely not occur to her to challenge it. Or perhaps rather she saw no reason to challenge it; her interests lay elsewhere.

I imagine Jane as having a strong sense of Christian moral duty to others without the need for conspicuous display of religious devotion ('value signalling' as the modern parlance has it) and, in common with Elizabeth I, having 'no desire to make windows into men's souls'. [1] In his memoir of his aunt, J. E. Austen Leigh says, 'I do not venture to speak of her religious principles: that is a subject on which she herself was more inclined think and act than to talk…'. [2] A simple, practical sense of morality, which although lying at the heart of Christian teachings, was derived as much from a sense of natural justice and fairness as from the church. (My father used to declare he was a 'Christian atheist'.) She was not the proselytising sort; there is no preachiness in her writings.

In January 1821 John Murray's periodical the *Quarterly Review* contained a review of Jane Austen's *NA* and *Persuasion* by Richard Whately (1787-1863), which includes the following:

> '…Miss Austin [*sic*] has the merit (in our judgment most essential) of being evidently a Christian writer:

a merit which is much enhanced, both on the score of good taste, and of practical utility, by her religion being not at all obtrusive. She might defy the most fastidious critic to call any of her novels (as Caelebs was designated, we will not say altogether without reason), a "dramatic sermon." The subject is rather alluded to, and that incidentally, than studiously brought forward and dwelt upon. In fact she is more sparing of it than would be thought desirable by some persons; perhaps even by herself, had she consulted merely her own sentiments; but she probably introduced it as far as she thought would be generally acceptable and profitable: for when the purpose of inculcating a religious principle is made too palpably prominent, many readers, if they do not throw aside the book with disgust, are apt to fortify themselves with that respectful kind of apathy with which they undergo a regular sermon, and prepare themselves as they do to swallow a dose of medicine, endeavouring to get it down in large gulps, without tasting it more than is necessary…'. [3]

We can imagine she would have enjoyed the majestic, elevated prose of the King James Bible or a well-executed sermon 'conveyed to the world in the best-chosen language' (to steal Jane's phrase from *NA* [4]) and I imagine she would have enjoyed the theatre of a 'fire and brimstone' sermon.

Church attendance as a social event would have much to offer: all human foibles paraded before her, either in overt display or in transparent hypocrisy, in unseemly fawning competition for status or position or favour, and in the merely cosmetic: 'Very little white satin, very few lace veils; a most pitiful business!' [5] Her relish for the ridiculous would find much to be amused with; as Mr Bennett has it, 'For what do we live, but to provide sport for our neighbours and to laugh at them in our turn'. [6]

A passage in a letter to Cassandra makes it clear that she found the absence of hypocrisy remarkable:

> 'Poor man! - I mean Mr Wither – his life is so useful, his character so respectable and worthy, that I really believe there is a good deal of sincerity in the general concern expressed on his account.' [7]

And it is clear from her novels (Mr Collins, Mr Elton) that she did not have unqualified regard for men of the cloth.

The first sentence of a prayer she composed speaks directly to her awareness of hypocrisy: 'Give us grace, almighty father, so to pray, as to deserve to be heard, to address thee with our hearts, as with our lips.' [8] In her writing, as in her prayers, she deserves to be heard.

REFERENCES

1. Oral tradition, the words possibly originating in a letter drafted by Sir Francis Bacon; in J. B. Black, *Reign of Elizabeth 1558–1603*, Oxford University Press, New York, 1936.

2. J. E. Austen-Leigh, *A Memoir of Jane Austen and Other Family Recollections*, ed. Sutherland, Oxford University Press, Oxford, 2002, p. 79.

3. Unsigned review but attributed to Richard Whately, *Quarterly Review*, John Murray, London, January, 1821.

4. *NA*, ch. 5.

5. *Emma*, ch. 55.

6. *P&P*, ch. 57.

7. Letter No. 18, 21 January 1799.

8. P. Hollingsworth, *The Spirituality of Jane Austen*, Lion Books, Oxford, 2017, p. 177.

JANE'S MANUSCRIPTS

We have manuscripts for the juvenilia, *Lady Susan*, the fragments: *The Watsons, Sanditon,* and Chapters 10 and 11 of *Persuasion*. No manuscripts survive for her completed mature works (although a case might be made for *Lady Susan*).

What a tragedy that this is all that remains. And how strange. It seems the manuscripts were thought to have no value once a book was published. We can understand Jane not thinking them of value to others, having no notion of posterity's interest, but it would seem a hard thing to let go of these precursors to the published works on which she had laboured so diligently. It seems Jane had no sentimental attachment to her manuscripts. Having prepared a fair copy, the working drafts would appear doubly redundant. And once a published copy was available, what would be the value in a fair copy? The more interesting artefact by far is the original draft.

The British Library provide on-line access to the manuscript chapters for *Persuasion* with a zoom facility and a transcript including all the edits; a wonderful resource allowing close examination of a working draft. (The Morgan Library and Museum of New York offers on-line access to the fair copy, in Jane's hand, of *Lady Susan*.)

The interlinear spacing was so tight that her descenders (particularly those from her f's) interfered with the line below; sometimes to the extent that words on the lower line would straddle the f from the line above.

There are no margins. Not, 'minimal' or 'narrow', - none. The text runs to the edge of the page and she splits words with a connecting colon on each line (rather than a hyphen) rather than leave an unused space at the end of a line.

The striking thing is the density of the text on the page; this does nothing to facilitate editing, which does take place however, with strikethrough of text and interlinear substitutions. With *The Watsons* there is also the curious use (three times) of material on a separate piece of paper cut to the required size and pinned (not pasted) in place. To this day we metaphorically 'cut and paste', we do not 'cut and pin', but pasting would not do where an insertion rather than substitution was required, and was presumably driven by a desire to maintain the integrity of the booklet format that Jane used rather than use a cross reference to a separate sheet.

The booklet format makes for severe difficulties when editing, as Kathryn Sutherland observes:

> '…the booklet represents a near tyrannical structure, one that closes off options and leaves the writer dangerously exposed: get it right the first time, for there are few opportunities for extensive reworking of description and dialogue, for turning back or reordering the story line.' [1]

Why then use booklets formed by cutting and folding larger sheets of paper? What advantages do they offer? Portability? Well, they are certainly more compact but hardly more portable than separate sheets of paper. Individual sheets do have a tiresome habit of becoming disordered; the booklet avoids that particular hazard. And they are perhaps more convenient for the page turning reader, if not the author. But for a working draft it does seem a perverse format. Possibly it was in part an aesthetic consideration; a booklet pleased more in approximating a finished book? Or was it that the compactness and relative robustness meant that Jane was able to keep them about her person for perusal if she should find herself at leisure? With uneven road surfaces I am uncertain how practicable reading would be when travelling by coach and horses, but it did happen, and there would be stops along the way:

'I had but just time to enjoy your letter yesterday before Edward & I set off in the Chair for Cant^y - & I allowed him to hear the cheif of it as we went along.' [2]

'You were wrong in thinking of us at Guilford last night, we were at Cobham…We did not begin reading (*MP*) till Bentley Green.' [3]

Given the absence of pocket pens, actual writing when travelling would be impractical unless using a pencil. Jane is known to have used pencil; a copy of her letter to B. Crosby & Co. [4] was drafted in pencil and overwritten in ink.

It seems Jane's practice was to substantially rehearse material in her head before committing it to paper. If she anticipated extensive revisions, she would likely have given herself more room for manoeuvre. (There are sometimes extensive reworkings of material however.) I think we may be confident that she had the plot outline established at the outset, or the reordering of material would have been a nightmare. The 'cut and pin' patching suggests she may have been reluctant to start a new draft and that the one working draft would eventually be turned into fair copy. Although this cannot have been the case when she transformed *S&S* from its original epistolary format.

Two reports from her nieces, Marianne and Louisa Knight, might be seen as supporting this notion:

> 'Aunt Jane would sit quietly working (sewing) beside the fire in the library, saying nothing for a good while, and then would suddenly burst out laughing, jump up and run across the room to a table where pens and paper were lying, write something down, and then come back to the fire and go on quietly working as before.

> 'She was very absent indeed. She would sit silent a while, then rub her hands, laugh to herself and run up to her room.' [5]

We need to be wary of making too much of these recollections; how often was this behaviour observed? Once? Twice? Routinely? It may be that these memories are coloured by a growing mythology. And the suddenness of the action points to the capture of an idea rather than of a finally resolved phrasing.

The hand is cursive, elegant, and disciplined. (Although in

her letters Jane was occasionally critical of her own handwriting). The lines of text are straight and even, although they occasionally turn down at the end to squeeze in a whole word rather than splitting it. The deletions are by freehand strikethrough.

Stylistic features include the extraordinary length of the cross bar on the stem of her t's, the occasional use of a Greek style 'd', and extended tails to y's and g's at the ends of words; traits she shared with Cassandra and her father. At first glance their handwriting looks the same. Cassandra and Jane were schooled together, so there is no particular surprise in their handwriting being similar, but the similarity with their father's suggests he had a significant involvement in their instruction (or was himself schooled in the same way!).

> 'The varieties of handwriting were further talked of,
> and the usual observations made. "I have heard it
> asserted," said John Knightley, "that the same sort
> of handwriting often prevails in a family; and where
> the same master teaches, it is natural enough. But for
> that reason, I should imagine the likeness must be
> chiefly confined to the females, for boys have very
> little teaching after an early age, and scramble into
> any hand they can get. Isabelle and Emma, I think,
> do write very much alike. I have not always known
> their writing apart."' [6]

We might substitute Cassandra and Jane, for Isabelle and Emma, as the representative females.

The sale in 2011, of her unfinished manuscript of *The Watsons* to the Bodleian Library provides the ultimate irony. That the very queen of irony should be the iconic feature on a £10 banknote,[a] £10 being the exact sum she was first paid as an authoress (for the copyright to *Susan*). That this manuscript should sell for the value of 100,000 of those banknotes, when the published version can be bought for less than one.

·REFERENCES

1. K. Sutherland, *Jane Austen Writer in the World*, Bodleian Library, Oxford, 2017, p. 130.
2. Letter No. 95 3 November 1813.
3. Letter No. 92 2 March 1814.
4. Letter No. 68, 5 April 1809.
5. D. Le Faye, *Jane Austen: A Family Record*, Cambridge University Press, Cambridge, 2004, p. 206.
6. *Emma,* ch. 34.

---

[a] Which carries a quotation: 'I declare after all there is no pleasure like reading'. (*P&P*, ch. 11) Of all the possibilities available to the designer, to seize on this piece of hypocrisy from Miss Bingley!

22

INTERLUDE - JANE'S DEFINITIONS

<u>Janeite</u> (noun)

The likelihood, since you are reading this, is that you are one: *a devotee of Jane Austen's works.*

The term is often thought to derive from Rudyard Kipling's short story "*The Janeites*" (about a group of World War I soldiers who were secret admirers of Austen's novels), but was first coined by George Saintsbury in his introduction to an 1894 edition of *P&P*.[a]

Kipling's story is very much in his own style and may not be to the taste of many Janeites but is in its distinctive way a tribute to Jane.

At times I have hesitated to embrace the term, in part because to a modern ear it can carry imputations (entirely unwarranted, of course) of excessive zeal and social dysfunction (á la 'Trekkie'), and also perhaps in laying oneself open to the charge of undue familiarity in the use of her

---

[a] He spelled it differently as 'Janite'.

Christian name.[b] But I am reconciled having since discovered that it has the implicit endorsement of Jane herself. In a letter giving advice on novel writing to her niece Fanny [1], Jane says of the characterisations Fanny is attempting,

> '...I like Susan as well as ever - & begin now not to care at all about Cecilia...You have been perfectly right in telling Ben of your work, & I am very glad to hear how much he likes it. His encouragement & approbation must be quite "beyond anything." I do not wonder at his not expecting to like anybody so well as Cecilia at first, but shall be surprised if he does not become a Susan-ite in time.'

Austenian (adj.) (not Janeian!)

Of, or relating to, Jane Austen. The term is used in the same manner as 'Dickensian' or 'Shakespearian', and allows comparatives such as less/more/most Austenian.

Janeitism/Janeism (noun)

The set of characteristics exhibited by Janeites.

Janeism is sometimes used but is also the name of an ancient Indian religion.

To my mind, a somewhat clumsy construction, particularly because the suffix '-ism' is also used to form nouns relating to illness, e.g. alcoholism.

---

[b] 'Austenite' will not do, being a metallurgical term for a particular form of iron alloy. Austenitic steels have no literary merit.

Incomparable (adj.) (As in 'The incomparable Jane').

Having no equal, above comparison. Seems fair enough.

Divine (adj.) (As in 'The divine Jane').

Formally, *belonging or relating to, or coming from God.* (Or, for atheists, would be so belonging if there were one.)

Colloquially, *extremely pleasing.* The default usage by atheists.

Samuel Beckett, the playwright (*Waiting for Godot*) wrote in a 1935 letter, 'Now I am reading the divine Jane. I think she has much to teach me.' [2] A view that is diagnostic of a Janeite.

Claire Harman cites the American novelist and critic William Dean Howells (1837-1920) as the first to use the sobriquet. [3]

REFERENCES

1. Letter No. 108, 28 September 1814.
2. Cited in D. V. Hulle, M. Nixon, *Samuel Beckett's Library*, Cambridge University Press, New York, 2013, p. 12.
3. C. Harman, *Jane's Fame*, Canongate Books, Edinburgh, 2009, p. 162.

23

JANE'S DEATH

Jane left Chawton on 24th May 1817, together with Cassandra, to move to lodgings in Number 8 College Street in Winchester, in hopes of effective treatment for her long-term ailment. She died on the 18th of July. She had made her will on 27th April, which seems to indicate that she recognised that death was in prospect.

Her death seems remarkable for the equanimity with which she faced the end; a quiet acceptance, supported by her Christian faith. We might suspect a prettified report that was enhanced for public consumption, but we have no evidence to contradict this report. Is this because there is no such evidence, or because it was effectively suppressed by the family?

From her time in College Street, we have a letter from the 27th May, to her nephew James Edward Austen, and reports of a second, from which extracts are given in Henry's biographical notice and subsequently in James Edward Austen-Leigh's memoir. In Deirdre Le Faye's collection, this second is identified as possibly dating from 28th May and as probably addressed to Frances Tilson.

There are so many other friends and family members that might be thought fully deserving of a letter, that it is perhaps strange that there are no more surviving. In particular, given the other letters to her niece Fanny, it seems remarkable that there should be none to her during this time. We have Cassandra's letter to her giving the news of Jane's death, but nothing from Jane herself in this period. Her last surviving letter to Fanny is dated 23rd March.

I believe we can expect any final note from Jane would be held as a keepsake by the addressee since, whatever their relationship with Jane, she was by then a famous authoress, and regardless of her celebrity, the disposal of a last letter would be too callous an act to be contemplated by anyone with any attachment to Jane.

So, it seems there was a period of six weeks during which she was too ill to write or dictate letters. And yet just three days before she died, Jane is reputed[a] to have dictated the poem *When Winchester Races*, of which this is an extract:

> 'Oh! subjects rebellious! Oh Venta[b] depraved
>
> When once we are buried you think we are gone
>
> But behold me Immortal! By vice you're enslaved
>
> You have sinned and must suffer, then farther he said

---

[a] As with so many other aspects, it is difficult to know for sure.
[b] Winchester was known to the Romans as '*Venta Belgarum*', the *Belgae* being a tribe that lived in the area at the time.

These races and revels and dissolute measures

With which you're debasing a neighbouring Plain

Let them stand – You shall meet with your curse in your pleasures

Set off for your course, I'll pursue with *my* rain.' [1]

It has been pointed out that in terms of rhyme, the second line calls for 'dead' rather than 'gone', and in some published renderings is so edited. I cannot believe Jane afraid of the word. Could Cassandra not bring herself to write it? I find that hard to credit also.

We cannot imagine she composed these lines whilst wracked with pain or nausea, and if we accept that she did compose them, then it seems she retained her wits (and wit), and so there must at least have been interludes when she was relatively comfortable. So why the absence of correspondence during this period? We cannot believe 'final goodbyes' to be beyond her skill and the simple manoeuvre of 'to be delivered in the event of my death' would have avoided any difficulty in causing what might prove to be undue alarm. Perhaps composing letters to those especially dear to her was too emotionally painful. 'Final goodbyes' too upsetting to contemplate? (Just the thought of them whilst healthy has me blubbing.) This might then explain the apparent discrepancy. Perhaps the whimsy of comic verse was a relief from the inevitable despondency due to her illness and, unlike serious letters, something Jane had the heart to engage with.

Cassandra's letter to Fanny announcing Jane's death shows how capable a writer she was herself. The letter is dignified and heart-rending in its capture of the pain of final separation from one held so very dear. It is typically only later in life that we come to any realisation of this; to the young it usually remains an abstract concern. This is as it should be.

From Cassandra Austen to Fanny Knight:

...Since Tuesday evening, when her complaint returnd, there was a visible change, she slept more & much more comfortably, indeed during the last eight & forty hours she was more asleep than awake. Her looks altered & she fell away, but I perceived no material diminution of strength & tho' I was then hopeless of a recovery I had no suspicion how rapidly my loss was approaching.—I have lost a treasure, such a Sister, such a friend as never can have been surpassed,—She was the sun of my life, the gilder of every pleasure, the soother of every sorrow, I had not a thought concealed from her, & it is as if I had lost a part of myself. I loved her only too well, not better than she deserved, but I am conscious that my affection for her made me sometimes unjust to & negligent of others, & I can acknowledge, more than as a general principle, the justice of the hand which has struck this blow. You know me too well to be at all afraid that I should suffer materially from my feelings, I am perfectly conscious of the extent of my irreparable loss, but I am not at all overpowerd & very little indisposed, nothing but what a short time, with rest & change of air will remove. I thank God that I was enabled to attend her to the last & amongst my many causes of self-reproach I have not to add any wilfull neglect of her comfort. She felt herself to be dying about half an hour before she became tranquil & aparently unconscious. During that half hour was her struggle, poor Soul! she said she could not tell us what she sufferd, tho she complaind of little fixed pain. When I asked her if there was any thing she wanted, her answer was she wanted nothing but death & some of her words were "God grant me patience, Pray for me Oh Pray for me". Her voice was affected but as long as she spoke she was intelligible...I sat close to her with a pillow in my lap to assist in supporting her head, which was almost off the bed, for six hours, — fatigue made me then resign my place to Mrs J.A. for two hours & a half when I took it again & in about one hour more she breathed her last. I was able to close her eyes myself & it was a great gratification to me to render her these last services'...[2]

REFERENCES

1. Cited in C. Tomalin, *Jane Austen: A Life*, Penguin Books, London, 2000, p. 272.
2. Letter No. CEA/1, 20 July 1817.

24

JANE'S GRAVE

Jane's grave is in the north aisle of Winchester cathedral and stands (lies?) in marked contrast to that of her sister Cassandra's or her mother's. These two are side by side in St. Nicholas Church in Chawton and have matching headstones that simply declare, 'In memory of…' with name, date of death and age. Cassandra died in 1845, her mother in 1827. Although separated by 18 years in time, it seems likely that it was their separation in space by only one yard that determined that they should have identical designs. There is no inscribed epitaph for either of them. Their graves are respectable enough but otherwise unremarkable. Whereas Jane rests within a site she shares with Anglo-Saxon kings and has a prominent position with a handsome inscribed marble ledger stone; she is not tucked into some obscure corner. It is a location of high honour, and yet given that those who might like to visit her tomb (her mother and sister) would be some 16 miles distant in Chawton, it might be considered cruel to have her interred so far from them. But if Cassandra did think this, she made the best of things. She wrote to her niece Fanny Knight:

'The last sad ceremony is to take place on Thursday morning, her dear remains are to be deposited in the cathedral - it is a satisfaction to me to think that they are to lie in a Building she admird so much - her precious soul I presume to hope reposes in a far superior Mansion.' [1]

She may have found satisfaction (i.e. comfort) from this, but that is not the same as saying the arrangement pleased her.

There was no pomp and circumstance to her committal; it was only attended by her brothers Edward, Francis, and Henry, and her nephew James Edward (son of her brother James). The convention of the time was that women did not attend funerals. This absence of an audience gives no justification for the grand setting; yet there would be significant expense. How are we to explain this? The Cathedral authorities were acquainted with the Austen family, but presumably that could be said of many families. Possibly there was a family feeling that her particular talents warranted a particular marking; reinforced by the proximate opportunity of the Cathedral. Or was this an attempt to assuage a degree of fraternal guilt? (Should have done more whilst she was living...) Would it be so outrageous to speculate that the Dean, Thomas Rennell, in whose gift the burial site lay, was himself a proto-Janeite?

In a letter to her nephew, James Edward, less than three weeks before her death, there is a double irony:

'Mr Lyford says he will cure me, & if he fails I shall draw up a Memorial & lay it before the Dean &

127

Chapter, & have no doubt of redress from that Pious, Learned & disinterested Body'. [2]

Deirdre Le Faye's annotation explains that in this context, 'draw up a Memorial' refers to 'a written statement forming the ground of a petition, laid before a legislative or other body' - so, a memorandum invoking the cathedral authorities in judgement of a claim against Mr Lyford. [3]

Her wealthy brother, Edmund Austen Knight, owner of the Steventon, Chawton and Godmersham estates, died in 1852, surviving both his sisters and his mother, and would seem the primary candidate for covering the funeral cost (£92). Since the residue of Jane's estate went to Cassandra, this would mean that any expenses paid from Jane's estate would effectively have been paid by Cassandra. I find it difficult to believe her brothers would allow their relatively poor sister, who was sharing a household with their mother, to alone bear the costs of a funeral that they could not attend?

The point is routinely made that Jane's gravestone epitaph[a] fails to mention her writings, but that strikes me as a superficial assessment. True, there is no explicit mention of her writing, but her authorship had not been publicly declared by the time of her death, her works were identified as being 'by a lady' – only her gender being acknowledged.

---

[a] This epitaph and that from the nearby plaque are given at the end of this chapter. The transcription faithfully reproduces the text, punctuation, line breaks, capitalisation, and abbreviations, but for practical reasons not the actual typographical fonts used or the text justification.

The testimony to '…the extraordinary endowments of her mind' carries an implicit reference to her work, since it invites the question, 'What were these endowments?' It might be argued that her epitaph kept faith with the anonymity conferred in the title pages of her published works.

It is not as though there was any wish to disavow her writing: an obituary published days later explicitly identified her as the authoress of *Emma*, *MP*, *P&P*, and *S&S*, and Henry went on to see *NA* and *Persuasion* published in a combined edition, together with 'a biographical notice of the author'. The sentiment, 'She wrote some very fine novels', is less encompassing than the broader one of admiration for 'the extraordinary endowments of her mind'. This testimony is to her attributes, rather than her works, and might, in that light, be considered more elevated.

A brass plaque in the wall near Jane's tomb (funded by proceeds from her nephew's 1870 memoir) neatly avoids this trap with the formulation, 'known to many by her writings…', which places the responsibility for any want of elevation with the reader.

J. E. Austen Leigh, in contrasting the anonymity of Jane with that of her contemporaries (including Charlotte Brontë), reported in his memoir (published in 1871):

> 'A few years ago, a gentleman visiting Winchester Cathedral desired to be shown Miss Austen's grave. The verger, as he pointed it out, asked, "Pray, sir, can you tell me whether there was anything particular about that lady; so many people want to

know where she was buried?'" [4]

Whether this story is true or apocryphal is really beside the point, which remains well made: Jane did remain relatively obscure for many years despite the grandeur of her grave site. (Who was this gentleman, how would his experience be relayed to J. E. Austen Leigh? Why would the verger tell this tale, which only becomes entertaining when it is seen as absurd? A verbatim transcription is not credible. I suspect invention.)

A third memorial is the window, dating from 1900, funded by public subscription and designed by C. E. Kempe. It includes the following verses from Psalms, taken from the Latin vulgate bible (here translated into English) as presented in the Cathedral's booklet:

> Come children (lit. sons) hearken unto me: I will teach you the fear of the Lord.
>
> He will guide the meek in judgement: he will teach the meek his ways.
>
> My mouth shall speak wisdom: and the meditation of my heart understanding.
>
> My mouth shall speak of thy justice [and] thy salvation all the day long. Because I have not known learning. [5]

The fourth, to my mind, strikes a particularly discordant note. One imagines that a great deal of effort went into the selection of these verses and yet only the third seems pertinent in the context of a memorial to Jane. I was prompted to research this further and quickly found myself in something of a theological minefield.

The fourth verse is variously translated with quite distinct meanings. I give a non-exhaustive sample below:

> My mouth shall shew forth thy righteousness and thy salvation all the day; for I know not the numbers thereof. (*King James Version*)

> My mouth will make clear your righteousness and your salvation all the day; for they are more than may be measured. (*The Bible in Basic English*)

> I'll write the book on your righteousness, talk up your salvation the livelong day, never run out of good things to write or say. (*The Message Bible*)

> All day long my mouth will tell of your righteous deeds and acts of salvation, though their number is past my knowing. (*Complete Jewish Bible*)

> I will tell of your goodness; all day long I will speak of your salvation, though it is more than I can understand. (*Good News Translation*)

> My mouth will tell of your righteous deeds, of your saving acts all day long— though I know not how to relate them all. (*New International Version*)

> My mouth shall shew forth thy justice; thy salvation all the day long. Because I have not known learning.

(*Douay-Rheims Catholic Bible*)

(A pitfall for those that have not known appropriate learning is that the Psalms are numbered differently, depending whether the translation is based on the ancient Hebrew or the ancient Greek text.)

Frankly, for the memorial to imply that Jane 'has not known learning' seems ungenerous at best (perhaps aiming for 'humility'?) but strikes my 21st century eye as offensive.

I wonder whether it was possible that the selection was made from a reading of the King James Version, which would be the one most widely known in 1900, and which could be seen as an oblique reference to Jane's early death and the need to reflect on one's mortality, and that this was 'reverse engineered' to the Latin vulgate version of the same verse, with the unfortunate consequence that 'forward' translation then yields 'have not known learning'? (The reader will have gathered that I am no biblical scholar and for all I know this may well be outrageous and unwarranted speculation).

The window also has the opening of St. John's gospel: '*In principio erat verbum...*' ('In the beginning was the word...') Surer ground I feel.

There is also a Latin dedication which translates as: 'Remember in the Lord Jane Austen, who died 18 July, in the year of our Salvation, 1817'.

The figure at the top is St. Augustine of Hippo, whose name is abbreviated as 'Austin'. At the time, this riff on Jane's

surname must have been seen as having all due gravitas, but
to the modern eye the pun seems at odds with the other
rather ponderous sentiments.

Jane Austen

known to many by her
writings, endeared to
her family by the
varied charms of her
Character, and ennobled
by Christian faith
and piety, was born
at Steventon in the
county of Hants Dec:
xvi mdcclxxv and buried
in this Cathedral
July xxiv mdcccxvii
"She openeth her
mouth with wisdom
and in her tongue is
the law of kindness"
Prov • xxxi • v • xxvi

Brass plaque inscription in the wall near Jane's tomb

In Memory of

JANE AUSTEN,

youngest daughter of the late

Revd GEORGE AUSTEN,

formerly Rector of Steventon in this County
she departed this Life on the 18th July, 1817
aged 41, after a long illness supported with
the patience and the hopes of a Christian.

The benevolence of her heart,

the sweetness of her temper, and

the extraordinary endowments of her mind

obtained the regard of all who knew her and

the warmest love of her initimate connections.

Their grief is in proportion to their affection

they know their loss to be irreparable,

but in their deepest affliction they are consoled

by a firm though humble hope that her charity,

devotion, faith and purity have rendered

her soul acceptable in the sight of her

REDEEMER.

Epitaph on Jane's ledger stone in Winchester Cathedral

REFERENCES

1. Letter No. CEA/1, 20 July 1817.

2. Letter No. 160, 27 May 1817.

3. D. Le Faye, *Jane Austen's Letters* (4th edition), Oxford University Press, Oxford, 2014, p. 467.

4. J. E. Austen-Leigh, *A Memoir of Jane Austen and Other Family Recollections*, ed. Sutherland, Oxford University Press, Oxford, 2002, p. 91.

5. M. Wheeler, *Jane Austen and Winchester Cathedral*, Friends of Winchester Cathedral, Winchester, 2003.

CONCLUSION

I suspect the most significant missing piece from the puzzle that is Jane is 'Cassandra-shaped'. The sisters were so very close and yet we have no surviving letters from Cassandra to Jane. We only hear one side of the conversation. Cassandra famously wrote upon Jane's death that, 'She was the sun of my life, the gilder of every pleasure, the soother of every sorrow, I had not a thought concealed from her & it is as if I had lost a part of myself.' [1]

We have every reason to believe these sentiments were entirely reciprocated by Jane. Given the combination of their closeness (both physical and emotional), and the fact that she had a very real literary talent in her own right (as demonstrated by her letters to her niece Fanny), it is inconceivable that she did not actively collaborate with Jane. She must have provided a sounding board and been the first proof-reader for Jane's efforts. There are also indications that Cassandra acted to facilitate Jane's writing by organising the household to defend Jane's authorial time and space. (Jane was also close to her brother Henry, but, although supportive, he had his own agendas to pursue in other areas.) Without this Cassandra-shaped piece, which I suspect had something of a heroic self-sacrifice pattern to it, there could not have been a Jane such as we have come to know; other cares would likely have overwhelmed Jane's talent. If

Cassandra's fiancé had not died and she had married, would there have been an incomparable and divine Jane?

REFERENCES

1. Letter No. CEA/1, 20 July 1817.

EPILOGUE – JANE *PERDONO*

Although her novels are often celebrated for their Regency elegance, to the true Janeite this aspect is a minor aspect of the value of Jane's work. The period setting is largely irrelevant, and per my introduction, I invoke no less an authority than the Enlightenment philosopher David Hume (a contemporary of Jane's – just, he died in 1776) in support of this assertion.

There is a fundamental 'rightness' to Jane's work that resonates with all decent upright human beings; the remainder, barbarians all, need not concern us.

There is a Mozartian lightness of touch, coupled with poignancy, in delineating truths that we have always instinctively known, but not being properly conscious of, would struggle to articulate. (Or do I mean that Mozart (another contemporary) had this Austenian quality?)

I think of the scene in *The Marriage of Figaro* where the countess forgives her husband upon his supplication: '*Contessa, perdono*', which in the film *Amadeus* prompts Antonio Salieri to say 'I heard the music of true forgiveness filling the theatre, conferring on all who sat there perfect absolution'. [1] Richard Will writes, 'The tableau of forgiveness transcends the drama to conjure an apotheosis of grace'. [2]

Reading Jane, I have this same sense of absolution wash through me. Jane *perdono.*

REFERENCES

1. *Amadeus,* directed by Milos Forman, screenplay by Peter Schaffer, Warner Brother Pictures, 1984.
2. *The Ambivalence of Mozart's Countess,* from Music, Libraries, and the Academy: Essays in Honor of Lenore Coral, Edited by James P. Cassaro, A-R Editions, 2007.

APPENDIX 1: CHARLOTTE'S LETTERS

I mentioned in Chapter 7 'Jane's Love Life' the often-quoted criticism of Jane from Charlotte Brontë; '…the Passions are perfectly unknown to her; she rejects even a speaking acquaintance with that stormy sisterhood…'. In contemplating this remark we are left with the impression that Charlotte Brontë was entirely dismissive of Jane's work, but that is far from the case. It is interesting to read the full letter from which the line is drawn and where we find a fuller, more nuanced critique of Jane's style. It could almost be Marianne Dashwood writing of her sister Elinor's manner! Here is a challenge for students of English literature: compose a fantasy reciprocal response from Jane Austen critiquing Charlotte Brontë's style; Elinor's riposte to Marianne's charges.

We must acknowledge Charlotte's own eloquence and I reproduce here in full those of her letters that have substantive content concerning Jane; they are in themselves a literary treat. I do not say we must acknowledge her as correct in her assessment; only that her argument is masterly in its articulation.

The following texts are transcribed from Juliet Barker's book, *The Brontës: A Life in Letters*, Little, Brown, 2016.

Letter from Charlotte Brontë to William Smith Williams, Haworth, 12 April 1850

'The perusal of Southey's Life has lately afforded me much pleasure; the autobiography with which it commences is deeply interesting and the letters which follow are scarcely less so, disclosing as they do a character most estimable in its integrity and a nature most amiable in its benevolence, as well as a mind admirable in its talent. Some people assert that Genius is inconsistent with domestic happiness, and yet Southey was happy at home and made his home happy; he not only loved his wife and children <u>though</u> he was a poet, but he loved them the better <u>because</u> he was a poet. He seems to have been without taint of worldliness; London, with its pomps and vanities, learned coteries with their dry pedantry rather scared than attracted him; he found his prime glory in his genius, and his chief felicity in home-affections. I like Southey.

I have likewise read one of Miss Austen's works 'Emma' — read it with interest and with just the degree of admiration which Miss Austen herself would have thought sensible and suitable — anything like warmth or enthusiasm; anything energetic, poignant, heart-felt, is utterly out of place in commending these works: all such demonstration the authoress would have met with a well-bred sneer, would have calmly scorned as outré and extravagant. She does her business of delineating the surface of the lives of genteel English people curiously well; there is a Chinese fidelity, a miniature delicacy in the painting: she ruffles her reader by nothing vehement, disturbs him by nothing profound: the Passions are perfectly unknown to her; she rejects even a speaking acquaintance with that stormy Sisterhood; even to the Feelings she vouchsafes no more than an occasional graceful but distant recognition; too frequent converse with them would ruffle the smooth elegance of her progress. Her business is not half so much with the human heart as with the human eyes, mouth, hands and feet; what sees keenly, speaks aptly, moves flexibly, it suits her to study, but what throbs fast and full, though hidden, what the blood rushes through, what is the unseen Seat of Life and the sentient target of Death - this Miss Austen ignores; she no more, with her mind's eye, beholds the heart of her race than each man, with bodily vision sees the heart in his heaving breast. Jane Austen was a complete and most sensible lady, but a very incomplete, and rather insensible (not senseless) woman, if this is heresy - I cannot help it. If I said it to some people (Lewes for instance) they would directly accuse me of advocating exaggerated heroics, but I am not afraid of your falling into any such vulgar error.'

Letter from Charlotte Brontë to G.H. Lewes, Haworth, 12 January 1848

If I ever <u>do</u> write another book, I think I will have nothing of what you call 'melodrame'; I <u>think</u> so, but I am not sure. I <u>think</u> too I will endeavour to follow the counsel which shines out of Miss Austen's 'mild eyes'; 'to finish more, and be more subdued'; but neither am I sure of that. When authors write best, or at least, when they write most fluently, an influence seems to waken in them which becomes their master, which will have its own way, putting out of view all behests but its own, dictating certain words, and insisting on their being used, whether vehement or measured in their nature; new moulding characters, giving unthought-of turns to incidents, rejecting carefully elaborated old ideas, and suddenly creating and adopting new ones. Is it not so? And should we try to counteract this influence? Can we indeed counteract it?... Why do you like Miss Austen so very much? I am puzzled on that point.

What induced you to say that you would rather have written 'Pride & Prejudice' or 'Tom Jones' than any of the Waverley novels?

I had not seen 'Pride & Prejudice' till I read that sentence yours, and then I got the book and studied it. And what did I find? An accurate daguerreotyped portrait of a common-place face; a carefully-fenced, highly cultivated garden with neat borders and delicate flowers — but no glance of a bright vivid physiognomy — no open country — no fresh air — no blue hill — no bonny beck. I should hardly like to live with her ladies and gentlemen in their elegant but confined houses. These observations will probably irritate you, but I shall run the risk.

To G.H. Lewes, Haworth, 18 January 1848

What a strange sentence comes next in your letter! You say I must familiarize my mind with the fact that 'Miss Austen is not a poetess, has no sentiment (you scornfully enclose the word in inverted commas) no eloquence, none of the ravishing enthusiasm of poetry' — and then you add, I <u>must</u>

'learn to acknowledge her as <u>one of the greatest artists, of the greatest painters of human character</u>, and one of the writers with the nicest sense of means to an end that ever lived.'

The last point only will I ever acknowledge. Can there be a great Artist without poetry?

What I call — what I will bend to as a great Artist, there cannot be destitute of the divine gift. But by <u>poetry</u> I am sure you understand something different to what I do — as you do by 'sentiment'. It is <u>poetry</u>, as I comprehend the word which elevates that masculine George Sand, and makes out of something coarse, something godlike. It is 'sentiment', in my sense of the term, sentiment jealously hidden, but genuine, which extracts the venom from that formidable Thackeray, and converts what might be only corrosive poison into purifying elixir. If Thackeray did not cherish in his large heart deep feeling for his kind, he would delight to exterminate; as it is, I believe he wishes only to reform.

Miss Austen, being as you say without 'sentiment', without <u>poetry</u>, may be — <u>is</u> sensible, real (more <u>real</u> than <u>true</u>) but she cannot be great.

... I have something else to say. You mention the authoress of 'Azeth the Egyptian': you say you think I should sympathize 'with her daring imagination and pictorial fancy.' Permit me to undeceive you: with infinitely more relish can I sympathize with Miss Austen's clear common sense and subtle shrewdness. If you find no inspiration in Miss Austen's page, neither do you find there windy wordiness: to use your words once again, she exquisitely adapts her means to her end: both are very subdued, a little contracted, but never absurd. 1 have not read 'Azeth', but I did read or begin to read a tale in the 'New Monthly' from the same pen, and harsh as the opinion may sound to you, I must cordially avow that I thought it both turgid and feeble: it reminded me of some of the most inflated and emptiest parts of Bulwer's novels: I found in it neither strength, sense nor originality.

APPENDIX 2: PRECURSOR ESSAY

JANE AUSTEN; ENGINEER?

Several years before I had any notion of writing a book about Jane Austen, I wrote this essay for my book on Professional Engineering. [1] It is not a good fit for the book proper but may be of interest to some...

I am pleased to declare that I am admirer of Jane Austen (in a moment of flippancy I did think to say 'confess' but that would carry a connotation of shamefulness which is entirely absent). There are those that would dismiss her literary canon as 'chick lit.'. but we need not concern ourselves with these barbarians, who are unlikely to make it past the title of my essay. The genius of Jane Austen lies in, 'the most thorough knowledge of human nature, the happiest delineation of its varieties, the liveliest effusion of wit and humour...conveyed to the world in the best chosen language', as one of her characters says of novels as an art form. The particular pleasure to be derived from her work lies chiefly in the intelligence and wit with which she draws the nicest of distinctions; only if it were merely a matter of Regency elegance and a study of manners might it deserve the appellation 'chick lit.' But let us consider whether Jane Austen had the necessary attributes to be an engineer – assuredly a piece of whimsy, but I enjoy the sport and might in the process establish some insights into the nature of these attributes.

Clearly, she possessed a remarkably fine intelligence: I conjecture that such intelligence would readily have absorbed the necessary learning in matters of physical laws and properties. I suppose there is the possibility that Jane was dyscalculic, which would perhaps have disbarred her from the heights of our profession, but I see no evidence for this or any other reason to doubt she could have acquired the required underpinning knowledge and understanding.

I trust the discerning reader will not need much by way of *persuasion* that Jane would not exhibit *pride and prejudice, nor th' anger* associated with an intemperate nature, but would remain objective and clear sighted. Engineering is often considered a *man's field,* largely I suspect because it is seen as requiring *sense* rather than *sensibility.* Certainly, as professionals we should seek to *emma*-ulate (ouch!) models of rationality and propriety, but it would be wrong to suggest that there is no place for sensibility.

Between the plain wrong and unworkable, and the indisputably correct and effective, there is a world of possibilities where the identification of the appropriate solution requires not only sense (to establish viability) but also sensibility to aesthetics and to context, circumstance and culture. Jane's novels demonstrate both sense and sensibility in abundance. Her particular talent was an ability to identify subtle yet profound distinctions and exercise proper judgement; not unthinkingly on the basis of a code (of etiquette) but from an understanding of first principles (of morality and humanity). I am confident she could have extended this approach to matters of engineering judgement.

There are those that see professional engineering as nothing more than the competent cranking of a handle on an appropriate mechanism (whether physical or procedural), and look to execute their allotted roles in this manner. Clearly there is a need for competent handle-cranking, in engineering as with any profession, but such a pedestrian view will not give rise to originality or intelligent and discerning execution. It is of course possible to competently crank a handle to no good purpose or to one that is poorly aligned with the proper objective. Jane's novels are not formulaic; certainly, her books inhabit relatively narrow territory, but they demonstrate a remarkable range of tone; the sombreness of *Mansfield Park* is in notable contrast to the gaiety of *Emma*. But Jane recognises the boundaries of her competence and does not stray.

Jane certainly demonstrated a mastery of language; something that some engineers affect to disdain, perhaps because they confuse poetry (as a celebrated but sometimes oblique form of language) and precision. But if we claim to value precision in our profession, we must logically extend this to our personal communications.

As a profession. I believe we like to lay claim to logic and incisiveness as particular attributes – none of your 'airy fairy' nonsense in our discipline. These are worthy qualities that in practice are too often distorted by political or self-interested motives. Jane would have delighted in exposing such distorted behaviour to ridicule. She is celebrated for the nicety of her language and, preferring the rapier to the bludgeon, she could use it in a most cutting manner. There is plenty of evidence for this in her private correspondence.

There is with Jane no self-indulgent ornamentation beyond the immediate purpose of her stories. She would have wielded Occam's razor with admirable zeal.

All very fine and pretty you may say, but could not the same be said of other celebrated authors, Dickens or Shakespeare say? I maintain not. Part of the appeal of engineering lies in the appreciation of form (whether physical or virtual) and function. There is a satisfaction to be found in identifying solutions which are fit for purpose whilst employing an economy of resource. There is also the appreciation of the harmony of forces or processes which inform our designs and empower our solutions. There is a poetry here that is an emergent property of our structures and systems. In Jane's stories there is remarkably little of the directly poetic. Although their subject may be romance, there is nothing romantic in their composition. She established free standing structures with a discipline and focus which yields poetry as an emergent rather than an intrinsic property. Like an engineer.

---

1. H. T. Dearden, *Professional Engineering Practice: Reflections on the Role of the Professional Engineer 2ⁿᵈ Ed.*, J. R. Smith Publishing, London, 2017, ch. 15.

BIBLIOGRAPHY

Fiction

Baker, J., *Longbourn*, Black Swan, London, 2014.

Hornby, G. *Miss Austen*, Century, London, 2020.

Norville, V. *Disciplining Miss Bennet*, Vivienne Norville, 2020, Amazon Kindle, accessed July 2020.

Non-Fiction

Adkins, R. & L., *Eavesdropping on Jane Austen's England*, Little, Brown, London, 2013.

Austen-Leigh, J. E., *A Memoir of Jane Austen and Other Family Recollections,* ed. Sutherland, Oxford University Press, Oxford, 2002.

Austen-Leigh, W. & Austen-Leigh, R.A., *Jane Austen, Her Life and Letters, A Family Record*, Smith, Elder & Co., London, 1913.

Barker, J. *The Brontës: A Life in Letters*, Little, Brown, London, 2016.

Black, J. B., *The Reign of Elizabeth 1558-1603*, Clarendon Press, Oxford, 1963.

Cassaro, J. P. (ed.), *Music, Libraries, and the Academy: Essays in Honor of Lenore Coral*, A-R Editions, Middleton, 2007.

Dearden, H. T., *Professional Engineering Practice: Reflections on the Role* of the *Professional Engineer 2ⁿᵈ ed.*, J. R. Smith Publishing, London, 2017.

Harman, C., *Jane's Fame*, Canongate Books, Edinburgh, 2009.

Hulle, D. V., Nixon, M., *Samuel Beckett's Library*, Cambridge University Press, New York, 2013.

Hollingsworth, P., *The Spirituality of Jane Austen*, Lion Books, Oxford, 2017.

Le Faye, D., *Jane Austen: A Family Record*, Cambridge University Press, Cambridge, 2004.

Le Faye, D., *Jane Austen's Letters* (4th edition), Oxford University Press, Oxford, 2014.

Mullan, J., *What Matters in Jane Austen?*, Bloomsbury, London 2012.

Quarterly Review, John Murray, London, January, 1821.

Southam, B., *Jane Austen's Literary Manuscripts*, Oxford University Press, Oxford, 1964.

Sutherland, K. *Jane Austen Writer in the World*, Bodleian Library, Oxford, 2017.

Tomalin, C., *Jane Austen: A Life*, Penguin Books, London, 1998.

Veevers, M., *Jane and Dorothy: A True Tale of Sense and Sensibility*, Sandstone Press Ltd, Ross-shire, 2017.

Wheeler, M., *Jane Austen and Winchester Cathedral*, Friends of Winchester Cathedral, Winchester, 2003.

Worsley, L., *Jane Austen at Home*, Hodder & Stoughton, London, 2017.

Bibliography

Internet Sources

Austen-Leigh, M. A., *Personal Aspects of Jane Austen*, John Murray, London, 1920, https://archive.org/stream/personalaspectso004072mbp/person alaspectso004072mbp_djvu.txt, (date accessed 12.10.2020).

Encyclopedia Britannica, https://www.britannica.com/art/novel-of-manners, (date accessed 3.10.2020).

Film

Forman, M., *Amadeus*, Warner Brother Pictures, Burbank, 1984.

Jarrold, J, et. al., *Becoming Jane*, Alliance Films, Montreal, 2007.

INDEX

accomplishments, 10, 11

Adkins: Roy & Leslie, 27

Ashe, 33

Austen: Charles John, 52; Edward, 27, 52, 89, 127; Francis William, 52, 87, 127; George (brother), 52; George (father), 53; Henry, 26, 27, 52, 55, 89, 101, 121, 127, 129, 137; James, 39, 52, 69, 127; James Edward, 121, 127

Austen-Leigh: James Edward, 5, 63, 99, 101, 121; Mary Augusta, 56

Baker: Jo, 82

banknote, 99, 117

bankruptcy, 27

banns, 47, 52

Bath, 39, 94, 95, 96

Beckett: Samuel, 120

Bigg-Wither: Harris, 39, 40, 41, 43, 44, 46, 90, 104

Bodleian, 116

Brontë: Charlotte, 36, 129, 141, 142, 143

Cadell, 13

Chawton, 62, 64, 71, 72, 75, 76, 77, 80, 97, 121, 126, 128

chick lit, 19, 147

Clarke: Stanier, 13

Darwin: Charles, 107

de Feuillide: Eliza, 37, 55

Downton: David, 100

Elinor and Marianne, 13, 26

Emma, 5, 10, 15, 34, 35, 42, 95, 96, 97, 116, 129, 142, 149

engineering, 147, 148

entail, 25

etiquette, 7, 18, 148

femme fatale, 54

First Impressions, 13, 26, 96, 97

Godmersham, 64, 67, 89, 128

Gretna Green, 47

handwriting, 11, 53, 116

Hardwicke, 47

Harman: Claire, 8, 96, 120

Hollingsworth: Paula, 52

Hornby: Gill, 61

Hume: David, 2, 139

Janeite, 74, 118, 119, 120, 127, 139

juvenilia, 14, 94, 112

Kipling: Rudyard, 118

Lady Susan, 13, 55, 56, 57, 58, 94, 112

Le Faye: Deirdre, 60, 121, 128

Lefroy: Tom, 29, 30, 31, 32, 45, 96

Lloyd: Martha, 72

magic, 14, 15, 16

manners, 14, 18, 83, 84, 147

Mansfield Park, 54, 90, 92, 149

Manydown Park, 39, 40, 79, 90

Morgan Library, 112

Mozart, 139

MP, 15, 36, 77, 78, 85, 90, 92, 114, 129

Mullan: John, 15, 16

Murray: John, 27, 107, 108

NA, 11, 46, 94, 97, 108, 109, 129

Norville: Vivienne, 20

P&P, 8, 13, 15, 20, 26, 36, 42, 43, 46, 82, 96, 117, 118, 129

Persuasion, 43, 65, 108, 112, 129
puzzle, 1, 137
Quarterly Review, 108
Register, 47
S&S, 13, 15, 36, 46, 115, 129
Sanditon, 112
Shakespeare: William, 67, 91, 150
Sheridan, 15, 90
Southampton, 94
Steventon, 33, 39, 75, 79, 80, 90, 128, 134
Susan, 94, 97, 117
Sutherland: Kathryn, 113
The Marriage of Figaro, 139
The Watsons, 94, 95, 96, 112, 113, 116
Tomalin: Claire, 11, 27, 95
Veevers: Marian, 91, 92
Whately: Richard, 108
Winchester, 3, 121, 122, 126, 129, 135, 136, 152
Woolf: Virginia, 19
Worsley: Lucy, 3, 74, 95
Zamit: Susie, 102, 103

ACKNOWLEDGEMENTS

This book is a family affair and I wish to record my gratitude to my daughter, Lucy Dearden Jones for the editing and keeping me on the straight and narrow with the referencing. Also, to my wife, Linda Dearden, for the portrait sketch of Jane and first proof reading. And to my niece, Alexandra Parkinson (www.creativechickensnest.com), for the book cover.

ABOUT THE AUTHOR

Harvey T. Dearden is a Chartered Engineer who works as a consultant in the process industries (power, oil and gas, chemicals, etc.; basically those with something in a pipe) and is also known to many through his active involvement with a number of professional engineering institutions. He has previously written two books on engineering matters and one on chess. He is married to an Anglesey girl and lives in north Wales. He has one child who is mum to Otts.

ALSO BY H. T. DEARDEN

❖ Professional Engineering Practice:
  Reflections on the Role of the Professional Engineer
  (2nd Ed.)

❖ Functional Safety in Practice (3rd Ed.)

❖ Crowns & Coronets, Mitres & Manes.

(Spot the chess book!)

Printed in Poland
by Amazon Fulfillment
Poland Sp. z o.o., Wrocław